Ask Carolyn

Straight Talk From the Dancing Divorce Attorney
~ Carolyn Woodruff

Practical wit and wisdom for today's family challenges. You can't make this stuff up!

ASK CAROLYN

STRAIGHT TALK FROM THE DANCING DIVORCE ATTORNEY

CAROLYN WOODRUFF

WOODRUFF
FAMILY LAW GROUP

Ask Carolyn
Cupcake Buddies, LLC

Cupcake Buddies, LLC
420 West Market Street
Greensboro, NC 27401

ISBN-13: 978-1-940010-16-8

Cover design by: Marilynn Barr

Printed in the United States of America

DEDICATION

To Dwight

My husband,
best friend,
dance partner,
flight instructor,
co-pilot,
inspiration,
lover,
and last, but not least,
fixer of my computer
when it is a bad puppy,
making this book possible!

A SPECIAL THANKS

A special thanks to the following:
Roy Carroll, Publisher of Rhino Times
John Hammer, Editor-in-Chief, of Rhino Times
Elaine Hammer, Managing Editor of Rhino Times

Without these fine folks, this book would not have happened.

For more questions and answers like you find in this book, please see the bi-weekly column in *The Rhino Times* named "Ask Carolyn...The Dancing Divorce Attorney." You can also find archived columns on www.rhinotimes.com and click on "columns."

ALSO, Carolyn is a blogger.
See www.northcarolinadivorcelawyersblog.com

DISCLAIMER

ABOUT THE AUTHOR

Carolyn J. Woodruff, is a North Carolina Board Certified Family Law Specialist with more than twenty-years experience in family law. She is the founder and managing attorney of Woodruff Family Law Group at 420 West Market Street, Greensboro, NC 27401. She is a North Carolina Certified Public Accountant and a Certified Valuation Analyst of business. She is a graduate of Duke Law School with high honors and she was Research and Managing Editor of the Duke Law Journal.

While Carolyn handles a full caseload at Woodruff Family Law Group, she spends much of her time giving back to the community by sharing her passion for ballroom dance. Ballroom dance was Carolyn's personal divorce recovery program. At age forty, she had never danced, but a former friend suggested that she try five things she had never tried before but had always wanted to try. So here's the bucket list: dance, flying, billiards, motorcycles, and scuba diving. Out of these, dance and flying became life changing. Carolyn, along with Alosha Anatoliy of Fred Astaire Greensboro, have become three time Fred Astaire Ballroom Dance National Smooth Champions and Fred Astaire Cabaret Champions. Carolyn and Alosha are Gold Best of the Best Show Dance Champions, and have made four appearances in the New York Show, *Dance Legends*. Carolyn also does showdance in the community, with her husband, Dwight.

Carolyn and her husband, Dwight Ensley, are co-authors of the children's holiday book, *The Seven Nights of Santa. Captain Green Eyes*, a black cat that flies a biplane, is the hero of the book. The book is for small children, their parents, grandparents, and caregivers. As an inspiration from the book, Carolyn started the Captain Green Eyes Dance Troupe, with the Boys and Girls Club in Greensboro, a free summer dance camp for children.

Carolyn also is a private pilot and enjoys flying a single engine Piper Cherokee Archer 180.

OTHER BOOKS BY CAROLYN WOODRUFF

~ *Ask Carolyn Two* ~

~ *The Seven Nights of Santa* ~
Coauthored with Dwight A. Ensley

CONTENTS

CHAPTER ONE

Alienation & Civil Actions

GENERAL OVERVIEW

Alienation of affection can relate to a spouse who becomes alienated from you, or to a child who becomes alienated from you. (See also Chapter Three on Parental Alienation). You also may have to defend yourself against allegations of alienation.

Alienation of affection is a cause of action you may have against your spouse's paramour. Detective evidence is generally quite important to this cause of action, and the detective needs to document that your spouse has been alone with the paramour in a compromising situation, such as a hotel. Also, the detective needs to document kissing, hugging, or other types of affection. Of course, there are other types of proof such as a confession.

Criminal conversation is a tort action against a person who has sex with your spouse without your consent. This is more commonly confirmed with detective evidence. You have three years from the date of the sexual encounter to bring the action. You are asking—usually a jury—to award you money damages. The amount a jury awards varies.

You may also be accused of criminal conversation and need a defense. There are many counterclaims and defenses.

◆ ALIENATION OF AFFECTION AND CRIMINAL CONVERSATION

Dear Carolyn,

My husband is having an affair with his secretary and I want to get that woman. I kicked him out of our home on New Year's Day when he made an excuse that he had to go by the office for something (something? Right?), and my detective caught them red-handed. I hear about alienation of affection. Do I qualify? How much do you think I'll get?

Wondering

~ Carolyn Answers...

Dear Wondering,

While you need to have a family lawyer go over your evidence, you may have a claim for alienation of affection AND criminal conversation against the secretary. Alienation of affection requires (1) that you and your spouse had a genuine marital relationship; (2) that your spousal love was destroyed; (3) that the secretary caused the breakup of the genuine marital relationship; and (4) that you have damages.

Criminal conversation does not have to do with any crime we actually punish today. The requirements for criminal conversation are two-fold: (1) sex (2) with someone's spouse. That's it.

No one can really say how much you might get. Juries generally decide these issues, and juries can really vary and view these issues differently. It is attention-grabbing that there have been some very large awards in North Carolina reported in the North Carolina Court of Appeals and North Carolina Supreme Court literature.

CHAPTER TWO

Alimony

GENERAL OVERVIEW

In North Carolina, you may be entitled to alimony if you are the **dependant spouse**. This means you are actually substantially dependant upon the other spouse for support or substantially in need of support from the other spouse.

It must be **equitable** to award the dependant spouse Alimony. Equitable is determined on the following relevant factors:

- Financial needs of the parties;
- Accustomed standard of living;
- Present employment income and other recurring earnings of each party from any source;
- Earning abilities of both spouses;
- Separate and marital debt service obligations;
- Living expenses of both parties necessary for support of each;
- Each party's respective legal obligations to support any other person.

Finally, illicit sexual behavior plays a determinative role in entitlement to permanent alimony.

a. If you are the dependant spouse and you engaged in uncondoned illicit sexual behavior during the marriage and prior to the date of separation, you will not be entitled to Alimony unless the supporting spouse also participated in an act of uncondoned illicit sexual behavior during the marriage prior to the date of separation.

b. If you are the supporting spouse, your spouse shall be entitled to Alimony if you engaged in an uncondoned illicit sexual act during the marriage prior to the date of separation (and the dependant spouse is not guilty of the same conduct.)

c. If both spouses have engaged in an uncondoned illicit sexual act, then Alimony may be denied or awarded in the discretion of the court after consideration of all the other circumstances.

◆ WHO IS ENTITLED TO ALIMONY, HOW MUCH, AND HOW LONG?

Dear Carolyn,

I thought my wife was having an affair. I hired a private investigator and he did not figure out anything, so I confronted her about the suspect. She finally admitted having oral sex with the suspect, but denies intercourse. I want out, and out now! Will I have to pay alimony? Paying alimony, under these circumstances, would make me very angry.

Potentially Angry

~ Carolyn Answers...

Dear Potentially Angry,

Prior to 1995, a dependent female spouse who had intercourse with a man could not receive alimony. The law was limited to actual sexual intercourse as we think of it between a man and a woman. In 1995, the law expanded to include many more acts of sexual misconduct as reasons not to pay a dependent spouse alimony. Under NCGS Section 50-16.1A "illicit sexual behavior" is defined as "acts of sexual or deviate sexual intercourse, deviate sexual acts, or sexual acts defined in G.S. 14.27.1(4), voluntarily engaged in by a spouse with someone other than the other spouse." "Deviate" is actually the word used in the statute, and includes same sex acts, as well as acts like oral sex.

If your wife asks for alimony, then you will need to raise as a defense her "illicit sexual behavior" as a reason to bar her alimony claim. It would be nice if you had a recording, legal if both are in North Carolina when the recording is made, confessing to the oral sex. You do not have to tell her you are recording if both are in North Carolina. You can use the recording as evidence in court.

There are two other things your need to know. First, you must not be guilty of "illicit sexual behavior" yourself. The law indicates that if both spouses have committed "illicit sexual behavior," then it is a wash and neither gets to really use the "illicit sexual behavior" as an advantage in the alimony case. In other words, you must be proceeding with "clean hands." The second thing you need to know is that if you forgive her you have condoned the "illicit sexual behavior." If you condone or forgive, then you have erased your evidence. Continuing in the relationship with knowledge of her "illicit sexual behavior" is frequently deemed forgiveness, so if you want to separate, now is the time.

◆ MEN GETTING ALIMONY

Dear Carolyn,

I am thinking about separating from my wife of 10 years. She is a doctor and makes a lot more money than me. I am a school teacher and make extra money coaching, but she still makes a lot more than me. Neither of us are having an affair, but I am pretty miserable. We are both thirty-three. She works all the time and I take care of our two children. I also worked for two years while she finished her medical degree. I hate to ask, could I get alimony as a man? Our lifestyle has been great, and I would like to maintain that lifestyle as best I can. Thanks Carolyn.

Alimony Seeker

~ Carolyn Answers...

Dear Alimony Seeker,

Very interesting question, but the answer is quite simple. Men can get alimony on equal footing with women, at least theoretically. This issue was resolved by the United States Supreme Court in 1979 in the noteworthy case of *William Orr v. Lillian Orr. In Orr*, the Supreme Court held that an Alabama statute that made alimony only available to women was unconstitutional under the Fourteenth Amendment of the United States Constitution, which provides for equal protection. An interesting twist to the Orr situation was that Mr. Orr did not want alimony from Ms. Orr; rather Mr. Orr was upset that women never had to pay alimony under the Alabama statute. Mr. Orr's argument that the statute discriminated against men won.

Some men do get alimony in North Carolina, but there are vastly more reported cases of women receiving alimony. Times are changing. I personally believe toward more men receiving alimony. The thirties age group has a fairly typical scenario in divorce of both spouses working, or at least no one has been out of the workforce for 20 years. Neither of you are out of the work force. Contrast this with divorces of persons in their late forties or fifties where one spouse did drop out of the public labor force to raise children—those dependent spouses who haven't worked publicly for 20 years generally receive alimony if the supporting spouse has the ability to pay.

The North Carolina statute for alimony was revised in 1995 and set up 16 discretionary factors the court should consider (NCGS 50-16.3A) for determining the amount and duration of alimony. In your situation, the significant factors that should come into play would be (1) relative earnings since she makes significantly more than you; (2) duration of the marriage of 10 years, probably gets you at most 5 years of rehabilitative alimony; (3) contributions as homemaker since you care for the children, although even with fifty-fifty custody you will likely receive child support.

While no lawyer has a crystal ball on what a particular judge might do, based upon the facts in your letter, the facts suggest that you might receive alimony for 4 or 5 years. You would receive child support if you have at least 123 overnights with the children, and it sounds like you may have a great custody claim for primary custody. The big thing you need to think about is how the separation happens. You do not want to simply move out of the home you are living in because this is the current home of the children. The person moving out of the home is a big issue for you because of the children and also because of the likely big mortgage you have, which you strategically want as an alimony expense. Good luck!

◆ MODIFICATION/TERMINATION OF ALIMONY

Dear Carolyn,

My ex is receiving alimony, which I obviously do not want to pay. She has a son, by another marriage, who is a heroin addict. My ex-wife began dating shortly after our divorce, and she seems quite entrenched with this guy. He stays over at my ex's on some weekends, but he does still have his own apartment. I know he has a key to my ex's house, and I know he stayed there four weeks when the heroin addict was in rehabilitation. My court order for alimony says that the alimony terminates upon cohabitation or remarriage. Will the court terminate my alimony? Is my ex cohabiting?

Sorry to be paying alimony

~ Carolyn Answers...

Dear Sorry,

This is a common societal issue in our current world. Luckily, our legislature has defined cohabitation for purposes of alimony as follows: "cohabitation means the act of two adults dwelling together continuously and habitually in a private heterosexual relationship, even if this relationship is not solemnized by marriage, or a private homosexual relationship. Cohabitation is evidenced by the voluntary mutual assumption of those marital rights, duties, and obligations which are usually manifested by married people, and which include, but are not necessarily dependent on, sexual relations." (North Carolina General Statutes 50-16.9(b) in relevant part)

Unfortunately for you, I doubt that the court would find that your ex and her boyfriend are living together "continuously" and "habitually." From your facts, the four weeks is really the longest continuous period and there were some extenuating circumstances, perhaps given the heroin addict. (Although it is not really obvious why the boyfriend would move in while the son was away for treatment, they also maintain a separate residence, which is a factor that goes against your position.)

Generally, the law suggests that to cohabitate one must be acting like he/she is married, without the formal paperwork ("voluntary assumption of those marital rights, duties, and obligations which are usually manifested by married people.") Note that a sexual relationship is mentioned in the statute, but sex alone does not equate to cohabitation. Joint bank accounts, sharing bills, and taking care of each other would certainly be "evidence" of possible cohabitation.

A typical cohabitation situation that would likely present a winning case is a situation where the ex and her boyfriend were maintaining only one dwelling, living together full-time, and sharing bills.

I would suggest you continue to monitor the situation. See if the relationship continues to develop into either cohabitation or remarriage. Best of luck to you!

◆ ALIMONY INCREASE

Dear Carolyn,

I have received spousal alimony since a 2003, under a court order that provides that I get alimony until my death. I would like to get an increase because of the economy. My ex-spouse has income that is three times my social security and retirement. His home is paid for and he owns three motor vehicles. His social security and retirement from a big local company is great. I received zero from this retirement after 38 years of marriage. He was in Management. What are my chances of getting an increase?

Seeking More

~ Carolyn Answers...

Dear Seeking More,

First, I do not understand why you would not have received at least half of his retirement in your property division trial. That seems very odd to me. You may want to check out why you did not receive your half of the retirement.

Second, you want to check with social security. Go down to the Social Security Office and talk with them. Generally, a person in your position would receive half of your ex's social security or yours, whichever is greater. The requirements are that your ex is at least 62; you were married for more than 10 years and you are unmarried now; and you are not eligible for a higher benefit on your own earnings record. Your divorce settlement cannot affect your rights under the Social Security law. Interestingly, this does not reduce your ex-husband's social security, but it may increase yours if you are drawing on your own earning record.

A judge can modify an alimony order under North Carolina General Statutes Section 50-16.9. The document a lawyer will need to help you file is a Motion in the Cause for an alimony increase, and you will need to show a substantial change of circumstances. This could possibly backfire if your ex responds with a Motion to Terminate Alimony, which is also allowed under the statute. Given the tenor of your facts, it seems that he still has the ability to pay and termination would not be likely.

A substantial change in circumstances is defined in case law precedent.

Generally, you must compare all of the facts in 2003 with all of the facts now. That means your needs and income in 2003 and your ex's needs and income in 2003 are compared with that same information today. The court then looks at the overall circumstances of the parties to determine if a substantial change has occurred.

You will have to fill out an Affidavit of Financial Standing that goes through all of your income and all of your expenses. An attorney would really have to look at this Affidavit of Financial Standing and compare it to the Affidavit of Financial Standing from 2003 to give you a reasonable educated guess on your chance for an increase.

You mention the economy, which suggests to me that you are saying inflation has caused your bills to increase over what these bills were in 2003. Hopefully, you have the Affidavit of Financial Standing from 2003 and can do a comparison of the costs from 2003 until now. For example, if you can show the court allowed you $100 for Cablevision, but the same Cablevision today costs you $125, you have a change for consideration by the court, particularly if most all of your bills have gone up through no fault of your own. A $25 change alone would not be enough, but if all of your bills are more than 2003, you likely have the required substantial change.

If you do not have a copy of the Affidavit of Financial Standing form 2003, there may be a copy in the court file. The alimony order itself may also detail the income and expenses you had then.

Also, another change the court might consider is the change of your income going down because of retirement at a normal retirement age. For example, if in 2003 you were a receptionist making $30,000 and today you are retired making less, then that is a change in circumstance in all likelihood.

After consideration of your changes and your needs, the court would look at your ex's reasonable needs and income. If the court deemed you had a change in circumstances and he has the ability to pay, the court should award you an increase.

Another consideration is that North Carolina General Statutes section 50-16.4 provides for reasonable counsel fees for a dependent spouse related to seeking alimony. You meet the dependency requirement because you were found to be dependent by virtue of the fact you have an alimony order from 2003. There are two requirements in addition to dependency. These are as follows: You must be entitled to the relief you are seeking and you must have insufficient means to pay the legal expenses of the proceeding. Further, your ex must also have the ability to pay your attorney fees.

Practically speaking, you might get an attorney to write a letter making a demand for an increase and request to open up settlement negotiations. Most ex-husbands would not be willing, but I would try. The leverage you have is that if he does not discuss this issue fairly with you, he might have to pay your attorney fees. If there is one thing a payer of alimony hates more than paying alimony, it is paying the attorney who got you the alimony. Good luck, and write back if you have further questions!

◆ TAX CONCERNS

Dear Carolyn,

My wife and I separated in June and I have been giving her $2500 per month for her support. I'm getting ready to work on my income taxes. Can I deduct the $2500 as alimony on my income taxes?

Wanting Deduction

~ Carolyn Answers...

Dear Wanting Deduction,

You do not say if you are paying the $2500 pursuant to a written, notarized agreement with your wife or a court order. Under the Internal Revenue Code, alimony deductions can only be taken if the payment is pursuant to either a written, notarized agreement or a court order requiring the payment. In order to make alimony deductible, the writing must provide that the spousal support terminate on the recipient's death and that the payment is made in "cash" or a "cash equivalent." The final tax requirement is that the payer and payee not live together.

If you do not have the required writing, you may want to approach your wife about filing a joint return. You were still married on December 31---as North Carolina requires a year of separation—so you are eligible for a joint return.

CHAPTER THREE

Child Custody

GENERAL OVERVIEW

The magic words in North Carolina in child custody trials are **"best interest of the child."** It is part of the Mission Statement of Woodruff Family Law Group to protect the best interests of the children. It is generally best for children if parents agree on a custodial schedule through negotiation and mediation. If no agreement can be reached, after hearing all the evidence, a judge must decide which spouse will make the major decisions affecting the child's life and will provide the child's day-to-day residential supervision. Except in unusual circumstances, the noncustodial spouse will receive substantial visitation privileges with the child. Rarely is a noncustodial spouse given less than alternate weekends, one-half of the school holidays and several weeks in the summer. There is no presumptive visitation schedule, and the court welcomes mutually agreeable visitation settlements.

Both child custody and child support are issues that can be raised at any time during the child's minority. Either spouse can petition the court to change its prior order of custody or support based on a showing by the moving party that circumstances have changed materially.

◆ SPRING BREAK

Dear Carolyn,

I am so stressed out over losing most of Spring Break with my children. Under our custody order, I get Spring Break with my children in even years. While I would like my children half the time, I did not get them half the time in the school year, only the summer. Family time is really important. We had a Spring Break vacation planned, a very nice vacation together! I seriously doubt if the makeup days during "Spring Break" are going to do the children any good as they are going to be frustrated with the partially missed vacation. Finally, the School Board gave us back two days, but what can I do to prevent future stress?

Stressed Out

~ Carolyn Answers...

Dear Stressed Out,

Your situation is unfortunately a very common one in North Carolina right now, and it is causing many, many family law clients concerns. In your situation, you will not get Spring Break next year either as you only get this time in even numbered years, so it will be 2016 before you have this opportunity for an entire Spring Break vacation with your children. Further, if your orders are like most custody orders, the other parent got all of the snow days that ate up a portion of your Spring Break with the children. The Guilford County Board of Education needs to consider how many court ordered custody schedules have been upset over snow days and the loss of most of Spring Break. It is a social and societal problem, as well as an educational problem. There was substantial stress among family law clients awaiting the school board's decision to give back the two days.

You have a custody order that is creating the unintended consequences. You are getting less time than the court intended for you to have with your children. So what do you do?

I would file a Motion before the court for clarification because I assume your order simply does not address snow days. If your order is less than a year old, you can ask for Relief under Rule 60 of the Rules of Civil Procedure. Your order needs tweaking. Some judges are more likely than others to tweak an order, but tweaking it seems fundamentally unfair. The snow day situation is simply not adequately covered in your order. Likely, your ex had Spring Break in 2013, all the snow days in 2014, and then your ex will have Spring Break in 2015. That is three straight years with all the days in question.

We do not know if this year was unusual for snow. You have several options in your Motion for Clarification, and your choice will depend on your preference. Option 1, you might ask for half the snow days in the future. Keep in mind snow days can create day care problems for individuals who have to work on snow days. Also, snow days can create transportation risks for the children. Option 2, you might ask that Spring Break always follow the originally published calendar for the school and not the re-published calendar after consideration of snow days. At least this gives you the time with the children, even if you elect not to take them out of school for a planned trip. Good luck to you.

◆ THE VISITING PARENT

Dear Carolyn,

I am a father of a beautiful 8-year-old daughter and a handsome 10-year-old son. I live in North Carolina, but the mother lives in California. The mother has custody, but the children will be visiting with me for the last two weeks of July and the first two weeks of August. While I don't have much time given the distance between the mother's house and mine, I really want to make the time count that I do have. I can take two of the weeks off from work, but I have to work two of the weeks. What suggestions do you have?

Dedicated Dad

~ Carolyn Answers...

Dear Dedicated Dad,

Making memories is the most important thing you can do with your children. Close your eyes a moment, and ask yourself, what do I remember from the summer when I was 8 and 10 years old? I have asked this question to many people and hardly ever hear about memories that include who did the child's laundry or took care of day-to-day living needs. I want to encourage you that you can make memories in this short time and you can even be a very influential parent if you use your limited time wisely.

You want to be a hands-on Dad with whatever you elect to do. When selecting the four weeks that you and your son and daughter will spend together, make sure that it is your children's best interests that are foremost in your mind. I would start with the children's natural interests and not your own. A Dad who forces his personal pastimes on a child who is not interested in the same things almost always will not create a great memory. For example, if you are a fishing addict, do not assume that your children will love to fish. You might introduce the fishing sport to your children, but do not take them fishing every day.

Vary the activities. Make a list of 10 activities that are age appropriate and make a game out of each child selecting the top three activities he or she would like to do this summer. Make memories by documenting the activities and achievements of each child with lots of photos and video. Also, consider making an activities journal for each child to take back to Mother's house. You might even keep a color copy for yourself, so that next time the children visit you, you can review the memories with the children.

Since you have to work some of the time, you will need to have some day camps, so pick these carefully, focusing on the children's pursuits in mind over your own.

Depending on your budget, take at least one trip that will be a "wow" trip, if at all possible. Document the trip with lots of photos and video and make a trip journal for each child.

Throughout the next year, refer to the pictures and the journals with the children when you talk with them or video chat with them.

All the best in the coming weeks making memories that count for this summer and beyond!

◆ 50B AND CUSTODY

Dear Carolyn,

I need some advice. Is it true that once a protection order under Chapter 50B expires regarding custody, the original joint custody order under Chapter 50 takes control? If so, can the custodial father be in violation of the Chapter

50 custody order? Furthermore, the custodial father won't let the child see his mother. Every time the mother tries to get the child for the summertime, the father won't let the child come.

The child wants to see the mother, but the father will not let him. Is that considered custodian interference?

Custody Issues

~ Carolyn Answers...

Dear Custody Issues,

Thank you for your question. Hopefully, we will get to the bottom of your woes. A Chapter 50B custody order is only good for a fixed period of time not to exceed one year. At the end of the fixed period, typically a year, the Chapter 50B custody order expires. If there is a custody order in the regular custody case when the 50B expires, the regular custody order resumes in effect. (See NCGS 50B-3(4). If the father violates the Chapter 50 custody order, the father can be held in contempt of court and the court will likely require the father to comply with the Court's order. Good luck as you pursue visitation with this child!

◆ DSS AND CUSTODY

Dear Carolyn,

I have 2 questions.

One, how can my wife and I challenge a DSS decision? The last time we talked I told you about the decision based on the 50B my wife put on me in 2008 which was dropped due to no evidence. DSS made a decision based on that, but when we were in court, DSS didn't have really any evidence because when asked to testify, DSS looked like a deer in head lights. Can we get the transcripts for that proceeding to show that the ruling DSS made was false? DSS got mad because we told them we want our lawyer present, so DSS stuck it to us. How can we get our day in court that we never had?

Two, can the father of the minor child use that ruling to gain full custody or would he have to prove that the child was getting abused? How can we overturn that false decision, and what action can we take?

Seeking Answers

~ Carolyn Answers...

Dear Seeking Answers,

DSS is not a court with a judge. The only way DSS can get a judge and an actual decision is to file a petition related to the child with the court. That doesn't seem to be what you are saying happened. Otherwise, DSS has to rely on agreements made with the parents. You do not say exactly where DSS testified, and I would need to know that to answer more completely. In what kind of action or court room were transcripts made? Please try to explain as much as possible about this hearing where DSS testified so I can understand procedurally where you are.

One problem you may have is that court tapes may not be kept from 2008 if you are just now trying to get these tapes.

An internal DSS decision or action might be used in a custody trial, but it is one piece of evidence for the court to consider in a custody trial. The Mother would be free to use whatever evidence she had to show facts regarding DSS. Either the Mother or the Father can file a motion to change a custody order for a substantial and material change of circumstances affecting the welfare of the minor. Your cause of action is in District Court for a Motion to Change Custody.

◆ GRANDPARENTS

Dear Carolyn,

I know I should have kept my mouth shut during the divorce, but I didn't. My daughter-in-law ended up with custody (not that it wasn't somewhat justified), but now she is taking it out on us and won't let my husband and I see our own grandchildren. We worked hard and saved all of our lives, and now we have time and enough money for trips to the beach, mountains, even Disney World, and would love to take our grandchildren, but we aren't even allowed to take them out for ice cream. As grandparents do we have any rights?

Would-be Spoiler

~ Carolyn Answers...

Dear Would-be Spoiler,

You are in luck! The judge in his or her discretion can help you. The glitter of Disney with your grandchildren may very well be in your future.

North Carolina General Statute 50-13.5(j) covers the rights of custody and visitation of grandparents. You will need to file a motion (a written request to the court filed with the clerk of court) if you cannot obtain the visitation with your grandchildren from one of the parents.

There are three things that must all exist to win your motion with the court for grandparent visitation: One, there must be a custody case between the two parents; and two, you are a grandparent or other relative with a 'substantial relationship' with the child; and three, there must be a change of circumstances.

Bring pictures of your grandchildren visiting with you and enjoying time with you before the parental explosion to the hearing on your motion. Write out the facts of how you used to visit with the grandchildren and why this has changed. See a family lawyer about your grandchildren visitation for help with the process.

As a practical consideration, you do not say anything about your son in your letter. Was he awarded visitation? Will he let you see your grandchildren during some of his time with the children? This may be a solution, as well. If he has been deployed in the military there are other solutions. Also, this answer does not cover grandparents seeking custody from unfit parents, which is a separate set of rules.

◆ CHILD CUSTODY EVALUATION

Dear Carolyn,

The court has just ordered me to participate in a child custody evaluation with a local psychologist. My children are seven and thirteen. I am a concerned Father, and the Mother has a new boyfriend that is "no good." This new boyfriend is terrible around my children, and he is even spending the night with the Mother while the children are there. I disapprove of this. I also think the boyfriend is drinking and driving with the children in the vehicle. What is a child custody evaluation?

Concerned Father

~ Carolyn Answers...

Dear Concerned Father,

A legitimate child custody evaluation is a complex process performed by a North Carolina licensed psychologist (PhD) under guidelines established by the American Psychological Association (APA). The APA adopted and published *Guidelines for Child Custody Evaluations in Divorce Proceedings* in 1994, which were updated in 2009.

Here are the typical stages of a child custody evaluation, where there are no sexual abuse or other abuse allegations.

1. **Initial interview of each parent and general information gathering:** The psychologist has an initial meeting with each parent and receives information from the parent, which includes general background, education, employment, family of origin, education, medical issues, stressors, and anything else of general relevance to the matter. Information gathering might be police reports, letters from attorneys, previous psychological evaluations, mental health records, school records, and similar information. Be sure to tell the custody evaluator about the boyfriend, the drinking, and your concerns in your first interview. The psychologist may decide to seek an interview with the boyfriend, and certainly the psychologist will gather information from the Mother and the children on this boyfriend.
2. **Test Administration to the Parents:** Most typically in our area, the psychologists use the MMPI-2 for objective testing. This test is comprised of 567 true-false questions. While there is much research regarding how to interpret the results, the test remains controversial for use in child custody evaluations, so the evaluator has to be careful with regard to the use of any objective testing.
3. **Interview of the children:** The psychologist will meet with your child.
4. **Observation of the children with each parent:** The psychologist

will typically have at least one session with each parent and the children, unless there are allegations of abuse. If there are allegations of abuse the psychologist may not select to place the child with an alleged abuser.

5. **Collaterals:** The psychologist will get a list of people that each parent requests to be interviewed. This list might include neighbors, school teachers, counselors, grandparents, and perhaps other caretakers of the children.
6. **The Report:** The psychologist will write a confidential report with the findings of one through five above. Then, the psychologist will make recommendations to the court for the best interests of the child. Normally, the parents are allowed to read the report in his/her attorney's office, but the parent is not given a copy of the report. The parent typically receives a copy of the recommendations section from his/her attorney.
7. **The Court:** The court receives the report and considers it, but is not required to follow any of the report. That said, many judges give great weight to child custody evaluation.

◆ CHILD AS WITNESS IN CUSTODY CASE

Dear Carolyn,

I am in a custody battle with my ex-husband. My nine-year-old wants to live with me. Can my nine-year-old simply tell the judge this, and then we are done with this mess? I have heard a child can talk to the judge in "chambers", but I am not sure what this means.

Favorite Parent

~ Carolyn Answers...

Dear Favorite Parent,

I am so very sorry that you and the Father were unable to decide together as the parents what is best for your child. But, if the parents cannot decide, a person in a black robe will make the decision on what is in the "best interests" of your child.

First, and I want to say this gently to you: generally, a nine-year-old does not have the maturity to make the decision of where he or she should live and what is in his or her "best interests." Cases of abuse and neglect are perhaps different, but you do not mention that the child is being abused or neglected by the Father. This answer assumes that there is no abuse or neglect of your child by the Father.

Second, the court does not give "final say" to anyone. The court hears the evidence and judges the credibility, maturity, and objectivity of witnesses, and then the court, in its wisdom, renders a decision. Given the age of your child, in my experience, the judge would give little weight, mostly likely, to the opinions of a nine-year-old on what living arrangement is best for the child. The court may even consider whether you were influencing the child against the Father, whether intentionally or unintentionally, and give the Father even more time to offset your influence.

Third, would the child be allowed to testify in "chambers"? Normally, when an attorney uses the word "chambers," the word refers to the judge's office or perhaps a conference room in the judge's area of the courthouse. Under the law of North Carolina, both parents MUST AGREE for the judge to talk to a minor in "chambers." If both parents do not agree, then the child must take the witness stand just like any other witness. The child would have to be "qualified" as a competent witness on whether the child knows the difference between truth and a lie.

When both parents do not agree to allow the child to testify in "chambers", I have had judges ask the parents to leave the courtroom and have only the lawyers for the parents and the judge and courtroom clerk present. While having the parents out of the courtroom is less intimidating, the parents are "technical" parties to the proceeding and have a right to "confront" witnesses with cross-examination under the U.S. Constitution.

In my opinion, placing a nine-year-old on the witness stand is only called for when that nine-year-old is a witness or victim of a unique fact, such as in abuse cases. One example would be that the child actually witnessed something, and perhaps no one else witnessed it. Your child's opinion on where he or she wants to live could end up back-firing on you.

I wish you the best as you seek the best interests of your child.

◆ MORE DSS WOES

Dear Carolyn,

DSS testified at the 50B hearing for the child. The father of the child subpoenaed DSS to court, but DSS didn't have anything and that is the problem. We didn't even get a DSS hearing to even fight it out. How can we fight the decision?

DSS Woes

~ Carolyn Answers...

Dear DSS Woes,

I would really like to know what DSS said to answer you more fully.

Custody can always be modified on a showing of a substantial change in circumstances affecting the welfare of a child. These can be position changes or negative changes. An example of a positive change might be that an alcoholic parent has been rehabilitated. An example of a negative change might be a parent became a drug addict.

You appear to have options, and your best option probably is to file with the District Court a "Motion to Modify Custody" for purposes of changing the current custody order. You need to discuss "changes of circumstances affecting the welfare of the child" since the order was entered in the case where DSS testified. Essentially, why do things need to change? You have to explain this in your motion. You need to get the assistance of a family lawyer with motion if possible. The court will permit you to do this *pro se*, meaning without a lawyer, but this is not that easy.

◆ MEDIATION

Dear Carolyn,

I have a two-year-old and a five-year-old, and I am separated from their Father. I am filing for custody and divorce. I hear I am going to have to go to mediation with the Father, and I really don't want to see him. I am not exactly afraid of him, but it sure is unpleasant being around him. Do I have to go to mediation, really?

Curious

~ Carolyn Answers...

Dear Curious,

You are likely going to have to go to a court ordered session of mediation to see if you can settle custody and visitation of your children with their Father. Hopefully, the mediation process will end with a settlement and improve the situation with the children's Father. Do not worry as you will not be left alone with the Father, so you should feel safe and "okay"

Mediation was added by the legislature to the custody statutes with five aspirational goals: (1) reducing acrimony; (2) developing custody solutions in the best interests of children; (3) providing parents with informed choices; (4) providing a structured, confidential and cooperative facility for discussion of co-parenting; and (5) reducing litigation and litigation of custody cases.

The court can waive mediation in rare instances, but you are not presenting the facts in your question that would allow a judge to likely waive mediation. Let's face it: you don't like the Father, and most people who are getting a divorce don't like the other person anymore and that is why you are getting a divorce.

However, there are several reasons under the law that mediation might be waived by the judge. The statute (North Carolina General Statutes 50-13.1(c)) lists several reasons the judge might waive custody mediation. The judge is not limited to these reasons, but most judges are not going to waive mediation without a very, very good reason. The statutory reasons are as follows: serious hardship to a party, voluntary mediation outside of the court mediation process, allegations of abuse or neglect of the children in question, allegations of alcoholism or drug abuse, domestic violence, and allegations of severe psychological or psychiatric problems. Finally, the statute suggests that the court may waive mediation if a parent lives more than fifty miles from the court, but practically speaking in Guilford County, mediations are being held by telephone, in these cases.

I urge you to go to mediation and make the best of it for your children.

◆ RULES FOR TROUBLED VISITATION EXCHANGES

Dear Carolyn,

Visitation exchanges are almost always awful for my eight-year-old, when the exchange is not at school. I am a Father with fifty-percent custody. I have Mondays and Tuesdays overnight. My ex has Wednesdays and Thursdays overnight. We alternate weekends.

When school is not in session, we meet at a local fast food restaurant. My ex almost always brings her new boyfriend with her, and he almost always says something "smart" or derogatory toward or about me. I have emailed my ex to stop these and I have asked her not to bring him. My eight-year-old hears this nonsense. What should I do?

Exchange woes

~ Carolyn Answers...

Dear Exchange woes,

Obviously, it is not in the best interest of your child to hear the adults around him or her bickering during visitation exchanges. Your child is part of both you and your ex, and as such, he or she probably is stressed to hear derogatory comments about his or her father. Visitation exchanges should be happy for the child preparing to spend time with the other parent.

Recently, in Randolph County the news has reported a tragedy at a visitation exchange from which we can learn. Mom and Dad both had someone else with them at the visitation exchange. The two other people got into an argument at the exchange, and one of the two other people at the exchange shot the other one (non-fatal shooting). Apparently, the child witnessed this shooting.

So, what should the rules be for visitation exchanges when the parents just do not get along, or there are other troublemakers, such as your ex's new boyfriend?

Rule 1: Troublemakers should not be at visitation exchanges, at all. Leave them home. If your ex will not do that, simply use a recording device (in North Carolina) to record the nasty comments. You, then, have evidence for court. (Note: I am saying "record" only if you are a party to the conversation and you are in North Carolina. Other states have different rules.) Then, file a motion with the court regarding the problem.

This might be a Motion for Contempt of Court, depending on what your court order for custody says, or it may be a change of circumstances for the Mother eliminating emotional abuse of the child at visitation exchanges. In my experience, judges generally ban non-essential troublemakers from visitation exchanges.

Rule 2: You, yourself, should always be pleasant at the visitation exchange.

Rule 3: Unless the child needs help with luggage, you should stay in your car. Keep the windows rolled up.

Rule 4: Try to park in a place where there are other people around who are not involved in your case. There may be safety in numbers.

Rule 5: Document, with your ex, your position that the boyfriend is an unnecessary party to the visitation exchange and that you think his presence is detrimental to your child. Perhaps she will think about the child and put him or her first. If not, you have some evidence of your reasonableness when your motion is heard in court.

Good luck with your motion, if you cannot get the Mother to take care of this, herself.

◆ NINE-YEAR-OLD AND UZI AUTOMATIC WEAPON

Dear Carolyn,

Now that summer is over and school has started, I am reflecting on the summer trip with my two children, who are 9 and 11. Their mother and I are divorced, and I am trying to make summer memories with them that will last a lifetime. This summer we ventured to the West Coast to see the sites. While in Flagstaff, Arizona, headlines hit about a nine-year-old girl from New Jersey, who killed her Uzi instructor in a place called "Bullets and Burgers" in Arizona. I think "Bullets and Burgers" is in Mohave County, Arizona. I was astonished, and of course, I didn't expose the article to my 9-year-old daughter. I am just curious if this could happen in North Carolina. What are the North Carolina laws on this? Do we have places like "Bullets and Burgers" in North Carolina? My ex is dating a guy who owns a lot of guns. Could he take my children to such a place?

Curious and Concerned

~ Carolyn Answers...

Dear Curious and Concerned:

You are referring to a story of a 9-year-old girl from New Jersey who was on a family vacation in Arizona. This story has received lots of attention in the legal arena and in legal publications. Her family took her to the place called "Bullets and Burgers". She was assigned an instructor and shot a single shot weapon without any trouble. The instructor then let her shoot an Uzi automatic weapon that shoots 600 rounds per minute. She lost control of the Uzi and shot and killed her instructor, inadvertently. No charges were filed and the accident was ruled to be an "industrial accident." I am neither an anti-gun nor a pro-gun person and I support the constitutional right to bare arms, BUT----My personal opinion: I do not know why any 9-year- old needs the experience of shooting an Uzi. I question the wisdom of allowing a 9-year-old to shoot any gun. What I do know is that this little girl is going to have a life time of trauma from this unfortunate event.

Now, I want to address your situation and questions. Yes, this could happen in North Carolina. Arizona prohibits the use of automatic weapons until age 8. North Carolina has no age limit with parental permission and adult supervision. So, theoretically North Carolina law permits machine gun training and "potty training" at the same time.

There are gun ranges in North Carolina that rent automatic weapons to children with parental permission and adult supervision. Apparently, the shooting ranges make decisions based upon the observable maturity of the child. I have to wonder if we are training these children so they can kill everyone in their high school. It is a studied fact that children exposed to violence are desensitized to violence.

In North Carolina, your ex-wife's boyfriend cannot consent to your children going to a shooting range, but the mother can. A custody order – either by agreement with your ex or in the discretions of the judge – can prohibit a parent from taking a child to a shooting range, allowing the child to use an Uzi, or having the child around weapons at all.

◆ FACEBOOK

Dear Carolyn,

My ex is all over Facebook about what she did with the kids during Spring Break. She apparently took some young woman with her to babysit so she could spend more time with her boyfriend on the Florida beach. She posted my little boy "buck naked" on the beach on Facebook. She posted her "babysitter—young woman" drinking beer with at least a dozen empty beer cans in the background. She posted a picture of her boyfriend and her entwined on the beach on a blanket. And to top it all off, she posted a picture of her new engagement ring from him, and we are not even divorced. I have filed for custody of the two children. She wants alimony. Are the pictures I downloaded from Facebook admissible? Can I make her remove the nude picture of my son as I am worried about perverts? Do these Facebook pictures help me in my quest for custody and no spousal support? I am frustrated with the whole process.

Frustrated

~ Carolyn Answers…

Dear Frustrated,

I will say, your ex is acting in particularly bad taste. Facebook obviously has taken the divorce court by storm, but can you use the pictures in court? I would love to hear from readers with Facebook questions in family law matters. The answer is that as long as you legally have the Facebook downloads, you certainly can use them, and you will likely be asked how you got the Facebook pictures. The real "no no" is to pose as an imposter to get them, but so many people have open Facebook accounts that it is usually very easy to get the Facebook posts legally without even asking for them from the account holder.

In the event that you do not have legal access to the Facebook page and you do not have a "friend" of yours who has legal access, then you can seek the Facebook posts through a Request for Production of Documents in the lawsuit you have with your ex. She may try to erase them, but there is a cache with the prior posts somewhere in cyberspace.

With regard to the nude picture of your son, I would suggest a simple step first. Either you or your attorney (or both) should demand that the picture be removed from Facebook. If that doesn't work, you can ask your attorney to seek an injunction mandating that the picture be removed. I agree with you that nude pictures of children on open accounts in Facebook invites pedophile stalkers of your children.

Your ex has shown some poor judgment for a mother in a custody trial. I ask my clients to not post on Facebook during the pendency of a case as these Facebook pictures and posts almost always surface in court. First, she apparently has introduced the children to a fiancé before she is even divorced, which the psychologists generally tell is confusing and bad for children. Second, she is on the beach with a babysitter who is intoxicated which shows poor judgment. Finally, the nude picture shows she is not really thinking about the problems of perverts in our current society. You are on your way to showing she is not placing the best interests of the children first, for whatever reason. You have some good material for your custody case.

Finally, alimony terminates upon an ex-wife's remarriage. Your facts don't say whether she was with this man before separation, so I will not address that; if she was having the affair before separation, she may not be entitled to alimony at all, unless you were also having an affair. Remarriage or cohabitation are a termination of support for a dependent ex-spouse.

◆ PARENTAL KIDNAPPING PREVENTION ACT

Dear Carolyn,

I am the father of two children, ages 10 and 12. The mother of the children lives in West Virginia, where she moved after our divorce. The children were born and always have lived in North Carolina. The North Carolina order for custody allows the children to travel to West Virginia for 5 weeks in the summer. Last year the mother did not return the children when she was supposed to at the end of the summer, and the court here held mother in contempt. She filed for custody in West Virginia last summer claiming fictitious abuse of one child, but that case in West Virginia was dismissed. Then, I got them back. I heard that this might be kidnapping under some federal law. Can you explain kidnapping and whether I have any right with regard to kidnapping if this happens this summer?

Frustrated and Looking for Options

~ Carolyn Answers...

Dear Frustrated,

With regard to parental kidnapping, I think you are referring to the federal law for Parental Kidnapping Prevention Act (PKPA), 28 USC section 1738A. The PKPA is frequently not well understood. The PKPA was enacted to resolve jurisdiction conflicts in child custody cases.

Clearly, North Carolina retains jurisdiction of your case and the mother should not have filed in West Virginia; that filing was frivolous. Essentially, under the PKPA, North Carolina is the "home state" of the children because of the existing custody order in North Carolina. Home state was established because the children lived here six months before the case began.

In addition to home state jurisdiction, the PKPA has three other types of jurisdiction: 1) significant connection; 2) emergency; and 3) more appropriate forum. Since there is a home state (North Carolina) jurisdiction, significant connection and more appropriate forum absolutely do not apply under the PKPA. Thus, the only other jurisdiction to consider is emergency.

You state no facts that make me think that West Virginia could get custody jurisdiction under the PKPA for emergency reasons, and I have seen this tried in certain cases. In order to have emergency jurisdiction under the PKPA, the mother would have to allege that the children were 1) abandoned; 2) a child have been subjected to or threatened with mistreatment or abuse; or 3) a sibling or parent of the child had been subjected to or threatened with mistreatment or abuse. It is usually the false abuse allegation that creates the temporary problem in the other state (non-home state). This is what temporarily happened in your situation.

Please note that most interstate custody disputes are resolved under the Uniform Child-Custody Jurisdiction and Enforcement Act, which North Carolina has adopted, which is similar to the PKPA. The PKPA is there if you need it.

◆ PARENTAL ALIENATION

Dear Carolyn,

Hi, how are you? I have a question, my wife and I wanted to spend time with my stepson this summer but the father won't let her get him. Can he stop her visitation?

Seeking Visitation

~ Carolyn Answers...

Dear Seeking Visitation,

Greetings. I am assuming there must be a custody order regarding your stepson that does not give your wife, the Mother of the child, visitation during the summer. If so, the motion your wife needs to file with the District Court is a Motion for Modification for the Custody of her child, based upon a substantial change in circumstances affecting the welfare of the child. She should ask for visitation in the motion. Tell the court in the motion why it is good for your wife to visit with her son. If there is no custody order, please write again. Good luck to you and you wife in seeing your stepson.

Dear Carolyn,

My heart is broken. The mother of my children has bad-mouthed me so much and talked about our nasty divorce to the children so much that the children won't talk to me or visit with me. She has poisoned their minds. What can I do?

Broken-Hearted

~ Carolyn Answers...

Dear Broken-Hearted,

Estrangement of a child from a parent is a huge problem in high conflict families. While psychologists differ in what label to assign, if any, to this problem, a book named Divorce Poison deals with the continuum of bad mouthing, bashing, and brainwashing ending in parental alienation (sometimes referred to as parental alienation syndrome (PAS). Psychologists, who differ with Dr. Warshak, may describe the alienated parent-child relationship as "in groups and out groups." There is a body of literature worth studying on "in groups and out groups" that are not part of Dr. Warshak's discussion.

As a family lawyer of many years, I can tell you that parent-child estrangement is very real and devastating in high conflict divorces. The damages to the family and the child are extensive, and these situations need special care by family lawyers who regularly handle high conflict divorces or unmarried parents. Divorce Poison has help for parents who are the "target" of the manipulative parenting of the other parent.

The hallmark of good parenting is the presentation by the parents of a united front to the children. The gold standard of good parenting is not to let the child know the parents disagree about something. In Parental Alienation Syndrome, one parent may be undermined by the other parent in virtually every aspect of the child's life. The "targeted" parent may become unworthy of even the smallest amount of regard or respect.

Generally, the alienation process starts with bad mouthing, progresses to bashing and ends in brainwashing. Malignant motives are generally present in the alienating parent. Revenge, anger and hanging on to hate are frequently motives. The personality disorder of narcissism can be a factor. Remarriage and third parties can also play a factor.

The key to your situation is that the children have to gain insight into the fact that they are being manipulated. Therapy may help, so you might ask the judge to order therapy for you and the children. You need to let the children know that you love them and that you are there for them. A letter to them memorializing your love for them and telling them you would like to see them would be helpful. You may also want to include a few photos with the letter showing good times. Memorializing the positive is important. Keeping photo albums of the good times you had with the child and keeping these good times in the forefront of the child's mind is key. Take great vacations with the child and create memories that will never fade. You want to ask the court to give you some extended time in the summer so that the children can "de-tox" from the alienating parent. While no one wants to involve a child in the parental conflict, when brainwashing has happened, it may be necessary in the conjunction with a therapist to educate the child about brainwashing.

If you find yourself the target of an alienator, you must have an attorney experienced and knowledgeable about alienation of the parent-child relationship. Sometimes careful negotiation and de-escalation are appropriate, but on other occasions litigation is the only answer; that litigation has to be planned carefully not to back-fire with appropriate psychological reports and witnesses. Alienators can be convincing, so careful corroboration is key. If the court agrees with you that the other parent is alienating, the court has the authority to give you complete custody of your children, and there is precedent in North Carolina that allows the court to do this to remedy this serious situation.

◆ PATERNITY

Dear Carolyn,

I believe I am the Father of a son, but the Mother is married to someone else. I dated Mother while she and her husband were separated, but now they are back together. We had sex during the time we were dating and the child was born 9 months later---perfect timing for the child to be mine. Mother and Mother's husband will not let me see the child, and quite frankly, hide him from me. I want to see my son. What can I do? I do not have any other children.

Bewildered Father

~ Carolyn Answers...

Dear Bewildered,

You have a chance for visitation, and here's what you will need to do. North Carolina has a very strong presumption that a child born of and during a marriage is the child of the Husband to the marriage. You will have to file a lawsuit asking for visitation and asking that the presumption be overcome.

There is a case from the North Carolina Court of Appeals that is very close to yours in many ways—*Jefferies v. Moore*. In *Jefferies*, the putative father (supposed or assumed father) asked for custody rights and won because he rebutted the strong presumption that a child born during a marriage is the child of the Husband. How did he do it? *Jefferies* showed the court that he had had numerous acts of unprotected sex with the Mother during the time the conception happened. In *Jefferies*, Husband and Wife were Caucasian, but the child in question appeared to have a mixed race ancestry, which also helped rebut the presumption. The Father was of a different race.

So in your lawsuit, you are going to need to discuss the unprotected sex that you and the Mother had, along with the timing issue. Proof of the separation of Husband and Wife may also help your case. You do not say if there are other characteristics of the child that are unique to you and this particular Mother, but if you have those facts, please use them as well.

Be patient with your case, as it is likely going to take some time. You may have to fight about something called "standing" because of the presumption that Husband is the Father. The *Jefferies* case I mentioned should help you with this issue of "standing" (the right to contest the issue). Perhaps you have some letter or card from Mother acknowledging that you are the Father. An email from Mother to you acknowledging you are the Father would be fabulous for your case!

Your child deserves to know a fine Father. Fight for this right for your child!

CHAPTER FOUR

Child Support

GENERAL OVERVIEW

The noncustodial spouse (or parent) will generally be ordered to provide child support by way of periodic payment to the custodial spouse. The court must follow the North Carolina Child Support Guidelines unless there are factors requiring deviation from the guidelines. If there are reasons for deviation such as special needs of a child or high income in the family, then the determination is based, in part, on financial statements prepared by both parents. These financial statements will be filed with the court. The court will then review the financial statements itemizing the incomes and expenses of each spouse.

A noncustodial spouse's child support obligation continues until the child reaches the age of 18 or finishes high school (whichever occurs last). However, if the child is otherwise emancipated, payment shall terminate at that time. A party, by agreement, may obligate himself or herself to make such payments beyond these time limits.

Both child custody and child support are issues that can be raised at any time during the child's minority. Either spouse can petition the court to change its prior order of custody or support based on a showing by the moving party that circumstances have materially changed.

◆ COLLEGE AND NO CHILD SUPPORT

Dear Carolyn,

My daughter just graduated from high school, and she is college bound. Her father and I divorced three years ago. Her father paid child support, but I understand child support is ending now as she is already 18. I thought her father would surely pay (or at least help) with college, and he told me last night that he was not helping with college. What can I do? Our divorce agreement says NOTHING about college.

College Help Needed

~ Carolyn Answers...

Dear College Help Needed,

This is a most difficult situation for you and for your daughter. Unfortunately, in North Carolina, parents have no legal obligation for support after the child is 18 and out of high school. Other States are different. For example, in Alabama, the divorce court can order college if the child's lifestyle and economic status would indicate that the parent would have paid for college in an intact family. Also, in Massachusetts, as another example, child support continues to age 21.

The only way a parent can be bound to pay for college is in a private agreement. At the time of your divorce settlement, the father and you could have entered into a private agreement, signed and notarized, that describes how the child's college costs will be handled. If you had such an agreement, the agreement would be enforceable by you. Frequently, college is difficult to negotiate because Father's feel that the child will "snub her nose" at the father if college is guaranteed by a contract. You do not say anything about the daughter's relationship with the father, and whether it is a close, loving relationship.

If the child's financial aid application requires the father's income, sometimes it is helpful to have a letter to accompany the financial aid application stating that the father will not participate in college expenses. I have written several letters like this in the past for clients who have no expectation from a parent of college participation.

Good luck with college for your daughter!

Dear Carolyn,

I read that awful case in New Jersey where the 18-year-old sued her parents for child support and college. What a tragedy! I have a 16-year-old daughter who paid close attention to this story. Could that happen in North Carolina?

Worried Parent

~ Carolyn Answers...

Dear Worried Parent,

In a word, "no!" You are referring to the case of *Rachel Canning, Plaintiff vs. Sean Canning and Elizabeth Canning, Defendant pending* in Morris County, New Jersey. Rachel asked for private high school, college expenses and legal fees in New Jersey. The New Jersey judge thus far has been wise in the case, and Rachel has not achieved much with her high profile lawsuit, except a lot of legal fees paid by an intrusive neighbor.

First, in North Carolina, unless a parent contractually agrees for college, a parent has absolutely no obligation whatsoever to pay for college. That is really the beginning and ending of the discussion of college in North Carolina.

Second, in North Carolina, child support ends when a child reaches age 18 unless the child has either 1) emancipated himself or 2) is still in high school at age 18 making good progress toward high school graduation. If the child is in high school making good progress toward graduation, the court can order child support until age 20.

Third, private school under the North Carolina Child Support Guidelines is considered an extraordinary expense and should be considered by the court only to "meet a child's particular educational needs..." The guidelines, however, apply to non-intact families. In the Canning matter, Mother and Father live together and are not in a divorce. I do not believe in North Carolina that the court could or would order private school for a runaway like Rachel Canning.

Finally, let's discuss legal fees. I think the legal fees claim here should be found in favor of the parents who have had to deal with what appears to be a frivolous lawsuit by a spoiled brat and some nosy, interfering neighbors. Under North Carolina law, this case would probably be viewed with a Rule 11 analysis for frivolous claims. If the court found no good faith basis for the case, then the parents could get legal fees both from the daughter's attorney and the daughter. I also think in North Carolina, the nosy, interfering neighbors could be sued by the parents for alienation of affection, and thus, for money damages. Providing more than $12,000 in legal fees for this brat certainly added fuel to the family fire.

The Canning judge made some very good analogies. Are we going to allow a 12-year-old to sue for an X-Box? Are we going to allow a 15-year-old to sue for an iPhone? Are we going to allow a 16-year-old to sue for a car? Parents have a natural and Constitutional right to parent their children. The US Supreme Court has long recognized this as fundamental and precious. North Carolinians, do not worry. This Canning case likely goes nowhere in New Jersey, and it will go nowhere here.

◆ TAX ISSUES

Dear Carolyn,

My ex and I share custody of our two children, and I pay child support to her. I have every other weekend, half the holidays, and two weeks in the summer. My ex doesn't work, but her new husband does. I pay all the money for the two kids. Can I get the dependency exemptions for the two children for 2013? I really need these deductions for my kids, and I pay the bills – NOT HER.

Needing Deduction

~ Carolyn Answers...

Dear Needing Deduction,

I feel for you, as the dependency exemption is worth a lot of money. However, you cannot get the dependency exemptions for the two children under the facts you describe, unless your ex will sign an IRS Form 8332 giving you the dependency exemptions. The IRS is very, very strict about this.

Under the North Carolina Child Support Guidelines, you do not have the amount of nights needed for the court to award you the dependency exemption under the Guidelines.

Under the Internal Revenue Code, the parent with the most over nights gets the dependency exemption of minor children.

At your next child support review, typically every three years, ask for a deviation from the North Carolina Child Support Guidelines and ask for an order from the court ordering your ex to give you the From 8332 to transfer the dependency exemptions to you. That is your best solution, if your ex will not simply sign the Form 8332.

Dear Carolyn,

My ex and I share the children fifty-fifty. We have three children. I make approximately $25,000 more than the other parent. I pay child support even though I have them half the time. Our child support order says nothing about who gets the dependency exemptions, and I get in a fight with my ex every year over the dependency exemptions. Who should get the three dependency exemptions?

Wondering

~ Carolyn Answers...

Dear Wondering,

First, you need to know that this is a heavily litigated area by the IRS in the US Tax Court. Second, as a premise, federal law generally prevails over North Carolina law on the doctrine of federal preemption (ie, federal law wins over state law in certain areas). Third, you need to know that the Child Support Guidelines and the Internal Revenue Code (federal law) have a different result.

Under the North Carolina Child Support Guidelines if the parent who receives child support has minimal or no-income tax liability, the court may consider requiring the custodial parent to assign the exemption to the support parent and deviate from the guidelines. Your ex receives child support, so the assumption is that your ex gets the exemptions. You do not say whether your spouse has minimal income so I cannot address this point. The good news is that your child support order does not address this, so you cannot be held in contempt of the court order for child support if you take the exemptions. A mere assumption under the North Carolina Guidelines should not be grounds for holding you in contempt. The order would have to be clear on the exemption issue.

Under federal law (Internal Revenue Code), you get the dependency exemptions under the tie breaking rule. The federal tie breaking rule says that the parent with the greater adjusted gross income is allowed to claim the dependency exemption if the children are spending an equal amount of time with both parents. Remember, I said that federal law controls over state law.

All this said, your ex and you will be explaining the situation to the Internal Revenue Services, if both of you take all of the exemptions. The IRS may even look into the actual overnights of residence with each parent even though the order says you have equal time. You should try to reach an agreement with your ex.

◆ ENFORCEMENT ISSUES

Dear Carolyn,

My ex is taking me back for child support AGAIN. All I am currently getting is social security, and I live with my elderly mother. I am broke. Can she do this? My child is 16.

Destitute

~ Carolyn Answers...

Dear Destitute,

Child support is reviewable by the court under certain circumstances as long as a child is only 16. I do not know the current order you are under or how long it has been since a review. Reviews, generally under the Child Support Guidelines, can be every 3 years, and otherwise when there has been a substantial and material change in circumstances.

I have three points for you regarding your situation.

First, social security is income under the North Carolina Child Support Guidelines.

Second, I suspect the other parent is receiving a social security check for the child related to your social security, which is both income to you and a deduction from the amount of child support your owe. That generally is helpful in a situation like yours.

Finally, and this may be the bad news: Free housing can be considered "income" for the child support guidelines. You may want to consider some form of fair market value rent to your mother.

Dear Carolyn,

I have a child support order for my child, and the Father has been held in contempt for failure to pay child support on more than one occasion. We keep going back to court over this issue. The father certainly has money for hunting and fishing trips he loves, and he has a new sports car. What else can I do to make this Father pay? Taking him back for contempt after contempt is getting old.

Tired of Court

~ Carolyn Answers...

Dear Tired of Court,

Ah, there is a law just for you. If a person willfully fails to pay child support, the district court judge can revoke his licensing privileges for failure to pay child support under North Carolina General Statutes 50-13.2. Under this statute, a "licensing privilege" means the privilege of an individual to be authorized to engage in an activity by hunting, fishing, or trapping licenses, regular and occupational, profession, and businesses licenses.

The child support payer must be willfully delinquent in child support payments totaling at least one month's child support. This is a requirement.

Most fishing and hunting requires a license. Driving a car obviously requires a license. So, these licenses are presumably very important to this man. This may give you your remedy of going after what he loves.

Essentially, you as the recipient of child support go to court and tell the judge about the recurring problem of non-payment of child support in a Motion under this statute. You ask that he be punished by revocation of his licenses. If the judge agrees that the non-payment is willful, then the judge can revoke his hunting license, his fishing license, and his driver's license so he cannot drive his new, cute sports car. The Clerk of Court then has the duty to send the revocation status to the licensing agencies. The payer then has a long process to ever get these licenses back.

Another thing the judge can do is order the revocation of the licenses and then suspend the revocation, provided the payer is current in child support. Something needs to get his attention as child support is a parent's most important financial obligation. While this may seem like a harsh remedy, it is a remedy for repeat offenders that will perhaps work in your situation.

CHAPTER FIVE

Divorce

GENERAL OVERVIEW

In North Carolina, an absolute divorce is almost always obtained on the basis of a one year separation. Once you and your spouse have lived continuously apart for one year, without resuming the marital relationship, either of you may obtain an absolute divorce. Attempts at reconciliation marked by isolated instances of sexual intercourse will not automatically end the period of continuous separation. However, instances of sexual intercourse and nights spent together may add to the totality of circumstances sufficient to cause a court to find that you have voluntarily renewed the marital relationship. Should a court so find, the twelve-month clock will be reset.

◆ DIVORCE DEPRESSION AND RECOVERY

Dear Carolyn,

My divorce was this year, and I have the holiday blues. I even think I might be depressed. How do I make this holiday happy?

Holiday Blues

~ Carolyn Answers...

Dear Holiday Blues,

First, I say: "The most important part of your divorce is your recovery." You will be okay. While you must find happiness from within yourself, there are some things you can do to lift your spirits on this, your first holiday as a divorcee. Take some time to pamper yourself, such as a massage or a pedicure. Get plenty of exercise; take a long walk. Find a friend and go to lunch. Try something you have never tried before that you have always dreamed of doing---now is the time. Watch your intake of food and alcohol.

Remember, divorce is a grieving process that goes through four stages---denial, anger, complacency, and finally back to normalcy. Be kind to yourself.

◆ INNOCENT SPOUSE PROTECTION

Dear Carolyn,

I think my husband and I may be getting separated and divorced, and I am concerned about our 2013 tax return, which has not been filed yet. The tax return is under an extension. My husband has a small business, and I have no idea if he reports all of the income in the business. I have heard that I can be responsible if I sign the return. He never gives me a copy. Do you have any thoughts on this issue? Do I have to worry?

Worried and in the Dark

~ Carolyn Answers...

Dear Worried and in the Dark,

This is always a tough decision, and the law that applies to this is called: "Innocent Spouse Relief". There are some things that you need to know in making the critical decision of whether to file a joint income tax return with your spouse.

First, you need to know that you do not have to sign a joint return, but if you elect to do so, you are potentially 100 percent liable for any income taxes, interest or penalties related to the return you sign. Yes, I said 100 percent, not 50 percent. You see, the Internal Revenue Code holds each signer of a tax return jointly and severally liable for all taxes, interest and penalties, absent a co-signer being an innocent spouse. So, to me, signing a joint tax return is always a big decision for a person with a small business. Contrast this with spouses who both have W-2 incomes from employment with third parties; if the only income on the return is W-2 income, then generally it is safe to sign a joint return properly prepared. You, however, are in the riskier situation with the small business.

Second, don't assume that you will be granted innocent spouse status with the IRS just because you don't know much about the tax return. There are many, many factors the IRS considers in whether to grant innocent spouse status to a person in your position. Note, it is easier to obtain innocent spouse treatment if you are separated or divorced because there are different innocent spouse standards applied to those who are divorced, as contrasted with persons married and living together.

You might Google IRS Form 8857, which is the form you file for Innocent Spouse Relief. Read through the form and look at the factors considered. There are many factors, but a few are the following:

First, the IRS considers your lifestyle as contrasted with the amount reported on the return. For example, if you are living in a big, expensive home and driving new cars and reporting $20,000 on the tax return, you need to find out where the money is coming from for this lifestyle that you are currently living and spending. The IRS expects that you make a reasonable inquiry. You need to require that you receive copies of any return you sign. Your tax return preparer must also give you copies of your returns for a reasonable copy charge.

Another factor the IRS will review is whether you have been a victim of domestic violence. One area of domestic abuse is financial control and oppression. While this will not likely get you a 50B domestic violence protective order in domestic courts, financial oppression is reviewed carefully by the IRS.

As a final consideration, whatever unpaid taxes are owed for 2013 will be a marital debt in your equitable distribution (property settlement); therefore, this is one factor going in your favor of filing a joint return, which is usually the least expensive filing status.

I would recommend that you consult with a family lawyer and with a CPA or lawyer skilled in Innocent Spouse Relief. Filing a joint return can be a very big decision. Likely the return is extended until October 15, so you still have some time to carefully research your options. Good luck!

CHAPTER SIX

Domestic Violence

GENERAL OVERVIEW

"50B": Domestic Violence Protection Order, known as a Chapter 50B under the North Carolina General Statutes

1. *What is a Domestic Violence Protection Order or "50B"?*

   Any North Carolina resident has the right to file for a Domestic Violence Protection Order, known as a "50B". A 50B provides protection from someone you have a current personal relationship with or have had a personal relationship with who does or has done any of the following to you or your minor child:

   - Attempts to cause bodily injury, or intentionally causing bodily injury; or
   - Places you or a family member in fear of imminent serious bodily injury; or
   - Continued harassment, as defined in G.S. 14-277.3A, that rises to such a level as to inflict substantial emotional distress; or
   - Commits any rape or sexual offense that is defined in G.S. 14-27.2 through G.S. 14-27.7.

2. *How can a Domestic Violence Protection Order or "50B" protect me and my immediate family?*

   Depending on the facts of your case, the court has the right to take the following action (50B-3 Relief):

   - Provide you with a temporary order for custody for any minor children that shall not exceed one year and order the alleged abuser to pay temporary child support and establish temporary visitation and prohibit overnight visitation;
   - Tell the police to remove the alleged abuser from the home and help you to return to your home;
   - Order the alleged abuser to stay away from your home, the children's school, your work place, friend's homes or any place where you may be using as shelter;
   - Order the alleged abuser to pay temporary spousal support;
   - Order the alleged abuser to turn over any firearms and prohibit the alleged abuser from purchasing a firearm;
   - Order the alleged abuser to pay for attorney's fees;
   - Order the alleged abuser not to cruelly treat or abuse any animal owned, possessed, kept or held as a pet by either party or by a minor child and/or give you possession of your pet;
   - Order the alleged abuser to do what you ask in court if the judge agrees.

3. *What if I am falsely accused of domestic violence?*

   You need to vigorously defend yourself and take the claim against you very seriously. You need to provide all the documentation and witnesses possible to support your innocence. Woodruff Family Law Group believes that a false accusation of domestic violence is a form of domestic abuse in and of itself.

   Woodruff Family Law Group and its staff continue to stand against any form of domestic violence and is an active business that annually supports Family Service of the Piedmont, Inc., Women's Resource Center and other organizations that stand against domestic violence.

◆ CHILD SEX ABUSE AND CHILD WITNESSES

Dear Carolyn,

I have a very young child who has been the victim of sexual offenses. Will that child have to testify?

Concerned

~ Carolyn Answers…

Dear Concerned,

It is always tough to have a child on the witness stand. There are many types of "child" witnesses. For example, a child might be the unfortunate witness in a custody trial. This response is limited to the child witness who is the victim of a crime, which is what your letter describes. Rule 601 of the North Carolina Rules of Evidence details the competency of a witness to testify.

The first question is going to be whether the child knows the difference between the truth and a lie; the testimony of the child has to be on a promise to tell the truth. The judge must make an independent finding after personally examining or observing the child, regarding whether the child understands the difference between truthfulness and lying.

In North Carolina, a child as young as four-years-old was allowed to testify, regarding sexual offenses allegedly occurring when the child was only two. *State v. Ward*, 118 N.C. App. 480 (1995). A five-year-old child was allowed to testify while sitting on her stepmother's lap in *Reeves*, 337 N.C. 700 (1994). The U.S. Supreme Court declined to review this case. A three-year-old was allowed to testify upon a promise to tell the truth, even though, at one point, the child said telling the truth was "bad". *Meadows*, 158 N.C. App. 390 (2003).

This should give you some background on the issue of whether your child will have to testify. If your child understands the difference between truthfulness and lying, the child will likely have to testify if the criminal case is tried.

◆ EMPLOYMENT 50B ISSUES

Dear Carolyn,

I am so very scared. I have been the victim of domestic violence, and I have to go to a hearing at the courthouse on the domestic violence. They call this a

10-day hearing. I have a new job, and I am also terrified of telling my employer I need the day off for court. What do I tell my employer? I am also worried my ex may come to my workplace and create a scene.

Scared....

~ Carolyn Answers...

Dear Scared,

The legislature has addressed your concerns. "No employer shall discharge, demote, deny a promotion, or discipline an employee because the employee took reasonable time off from work to obtain or attempt to obtain relief" under Chapter 50B related to domestic violence. NCGS 50B-5.5.

You, as the employee must follow your employer's usual time off policy and procedure, including advance notice to your employer. So, tell the employer about the court date as soon as you know the date.

The employer may require documentation of the emergency, particularly if it causes you not to be able to comply with the usual time off policy of the employer.

When you are at court at your 50B hearing, please ask the judge to prohibit your ex from coming to your workplace. Frequently, when a 50B is granted, the defendant is prohibited from going to the victim's workplace, as well as any other defined place the victim frequents.

I believe your employer will be pleased with your efforts to protect yourself. Personally, I would want an employee to tell me of the danger, because these perpetrators may show up at your place of employment; it would be good for your employer to have safe guards in place in the event this happens.

Actually, an employer can get a 50C no-contact order regarding outside persons who are creating a fray at a workplace or victimizing an employee.

Best of luck to you in this matter. Please let me know how this turns out.

◆ DSS AND 50B

Dear Carolyn,

My wife and I need some advice. In 2009, we had to see a judge in a matter of a 50B taken out by my stepson's father based upon alleged child abuse. The 50B judge said that we would revisit the 50B issue after DSS finished their investigation, but it was never resolved. The father of my stepson let him stay with us after it happened. We waited a month, and the father's lawyer withdrew. The Judge dropped the 50B case due to the father not moving forward with the 50B. I checked a box on a DSS form saying that I was not admitting any guilt with DSS. DSS never did an investigation. DSS apparently found abuse in the home because a year before (2008) my wife got mad, and took out a 50B on me. My wife then dropped the 50B. Then, my stepson's father got a hold of the 50B my wife filed and dropped, and DSS went with the decision based on my wife's 50B. Can DSS base a case on my wife's dropped 50B?

Confused by DSS

~ Carolyn Answers...

Dear Confused by DSS,

The short answer is that it is unlikely the Department of Social Services (DSS) is relying on an old, dropped 50B (domestic violence action) without other evidence of alleged child abuse. DSS does keep a cumulative file on a family once a complaint is received, but each new allegation is independently investigated. Most often, DSS will talk with the alleged child victim at school or other location without any caregiver present.

Unfortunately, you seem to be the victim of a very convoluted and vindictive set of facts involving two distinct and separate legal processes: 1) 50B which is domestic violence in the court system, and 2) a Child Protective Services investigation by DSS (Department of Social Services)..."

Your fact pattern, as I understand it from your letter, describes three factual events in the following chronological order: 1) your wife got mad and brought a 50B (domestic violence action) which was dropped by your wife; 2) your wife has a minor child by a former relationship, and subsequently in 2009, the father of the minor child brought a 50B against you; in addition there was a social services (DSS) investigation regarding child abuse of the minor child; interestingly enough, the child came to live with you; 3) finally, and perhaps more currently, a child protective services investigation by Department of Social Services, related to the minor child, may still be pending. This seems to be your main concern, and you wonder how the historic facts are affecting your current situation.

1. The first 50B seems to be an abuse of the 50B system; 50Bs are not for mere marital arguments, if that is the nature of your wife's 50B. Getting "mad" is not a legal ground for a 50B. Taking out a 50B should not be done lightly, and should only be done in serious matters. Your wife did the right thing in dropping this first 50B.
2. While 50Bs (domestic violence court actions) are certainly necessary, they can be abused and frequently used for "one-ups-man-ship" in a custody battle. Your 2009 fact pattern suggests that perhaps custody was a motivating factor in the first 50B and the first Department of Social Services investigation, since the minor child came to live with you. It is hard to say from the fact pattern what happened to the second 50B, but 50Bs are only good for one year unless they are renewed. Further, it is hard to say if the second 50B was granted and expired, or never granted and simply died a procedural death at the courthouse, which could be related to the withdrawal of the attorney. I would suggest you make a trip to the Guilford County Courthouse and get a copy of that 50B file and see what happened to it. While you are at the Clerk of Court, you should also examine the first 50B court file to make sure that the dismissal by your wife is correctly stated in the court file. These are public records and the Clerk of Court must show you the court files on these 50Bs and give you a copy for a small copy charge. Armed with this information, you can see what actually happened with the first and second 50B. You may also want to show the two dismissals, if that is what happened, to DSS and make sure DSS has a copy for its file of the dismissals. Additionally, you also want to make sure you get a copy of the signed document from DSS. I invite you to write again if this gives you more factual information.
3. More importantly, let's discuss the current DSS investigation. First, you need to know that anyone can pick up the phone and make a confidential report to DSS of the alleged abuse or neglect of a minor child. Certain persons, such as medical doctors and psychologists, are ethically obligated to make a report of suspected child abuse or neglect.
   a. It is unlikely that DSS will rely on data as old as 2009 in establishing abuse or neglect in a 2013 case. DSS likely has a cumulative file

on your family and the particular minor child in question. However, DSS is likely investigating the current allegation of abuse independently of anything that has happened in the past. While obviously, the old files may provide hints of tendencies toward child abuse, DSS is going to rely more on current and independent evidence. DSS will interview the minor child, probably at school, with no notice to anyone to get the minor child's statement free of influence of any adult that might be involved. Further, DSS will evaluate eye witness accounts of others---such as siblings, other adults, and neighbors. DSS will evaluate medical records, and other evidence of physical harm (eg bruises), such as photographs. DSS, on occasion, even has studies done on families by mental health professionals.

Your biggest problem is properly presenting your position regarding the facts of the current DSS investigation, not the old files from 2009. If the current allegations to DSS are totally false, you may be in a quagmire of repetitive false reporting that often accompanies custody cases, and DSS is generally very alert to false charges to gain advantage in custody cases. DSS is a very powerful agency with regard to children. Many times, DSS will do an investigation and make a finding such as abuse or neglect and recommend services and safety plans. If these services and safety plans are followed, then DSS will not generally file a petition with the court for removal of the minor child from the home. However, DSS can file a petition with the court to have the judge remove the minor child from the home of the mother or the father. If mother and/or father are indigent, they are entitled to court appointed lawyers.

My overall advice is that you should concentrate on the facts of the current case before DSS. I do not know how serious the allegations are, but consider a family lawyer skilled in DSS representation. Good luck to you, and thanks for "Asking Carolyn."

◆ DEFENDING AGAINST A FALSE CHARGE

Dear Carolyn,

My wife keeps threatening me with a 50B. We do argue, but I have never laid a hand on her or even threatened her. She says in court it will be her word against mine. Is there anything I can do to protect myself? I don't want to go to jail.

Threatened

~ Carolyn Answers...

Dear Threatened,

Defending the innocent man in a 50B is a thorny problem, and not a bed of red roses. On these facts, you need something that turns the matter into not simply "her word against yours." You have to proceed with extreme caution.

1. Do not let her engage you in an argument. Walk away. Do not respond when she starts an argument.
2. Do not argue with her. Don't say anything; don't even throw a paper clip. If you are angry or emotionally charged over issues, you may want to figure out with a counselor how to get control of your emotions.
3. Wouldn't you love to have the judge listen to a recording of her saying: "Well, it will be your word against mine"? Use a smartphone application to keep a recording device going when you are around her; some apps will record for up to 10 hours. It is legal in North Carolina to record if you are both party to the conversation and both of you are in North Carolina. Please note that I said you must be a party to the recorded conversation. And, you cannot tap the phone or leave the recorder around, or otherwise record. You and the person you are recording must both be in North Carolina as the rules are different in other states. Illegally recording can get you in big trouble. If you are in doubt, check with an attorney on whether your recording plan is legal before you record.
4. If it is bad enough to have to record what she is saying to you, you need to consider whether separation is your best solution. Let's face it – spouses who are threatening 50B's, especially false ones, should be on the way out. Do you really want to be married to her? Since there are

consequences to moving out, please see a family lawyer before you move.

5. A 50B protective order against a defendant is a serious matter for the defendant. You will likely have to surrender firearms. You will be entered by the Sheriff of Guilford County into the National Crime Information Center as a person with a domestic violence protective order against him. This can affect background checks in future employment.
6. Information regarding the crime of assault on a female is not discussed in this answer, and the criminal charge of assault on a female may occur at the same time as a 50B complaint against you. This can send you to jail for 48 hours, or more.
7. A domestic violence protective order (50B) against you does not send you to jail unless you violate the 50B order. So if you get a 50B against you, do not contact your wife – do not even send her a dozen red roses – that would likely be an unwelcomed contact that sends you to jail.

◆ NFL DOMESTIC VIOLENCE, ARMSTRONG, AND TANNER

Dear Carolyn,

I am writing to you about the Ray Rice case and the new NFL Domestic Violence Policy. What do you think about the new policy, and could Ray Rice have gotten off this easily in North Carolina? I understand he is going to counseling and getting off the criminal charge of knocking his fiancée unconscious. And, the NFL only suspended him for two games .

Disgusted

~ Carolyn Answers...

Dear Disgusted,

First, domestic violence is a very serious and real problem, and people die in domestic violence situations. Look at the many cases from Guilford County alone, in the last twelve months, from Ms. Bianca Tanner to Mrs. Laurrissa Armstrong---both dead.

Second, our heroes in society need to reflect the values we want to instill in society as a whole, especially when we consider what is in the best interest of our children. If "heroes" are going to have the celebrity status of a football player for the NFL, they need to be good role models. We, as a society need to have a strong value of "no tolerance" for domestic abuse---NONE. The original NFL policy certainly did not do that. Baltimore Ravens running back, Ray Rice was accused of aggravated assault causing serious bodily injury after his fiancée was allegedly knocked unconscious, as I understand the situation. Surveillance video showed Rice dragging his fiancée, Janay Palmer, who appeared unconscious, out of the elevator. In July, the NFL said that Rice had to sit out of two games for his actions. This did not sit well with the national public, nor did it with some of the NFL owners, according to ESPN.com.

This led to NFL Commissioner Roger Goodell's revision to the policy in late August, which begs the question, is the newly revised policy strong enough?

The new August policy is as follows:

> Effective immediately, any NFL employee---not just a player---who is found to have engaged in assault, battery, domestic violence or sexual assault, that involves physical force, will be suspended without pay for six games for the first offense. Second-time offenders will be banished from the league. The second-time offenders can petition the league for reinstatement after one year, with no presumption or guarantee of reinstatement.

While this August 2014 policy is better than the slap on the wrist Ray Rice received, it is insufficient as a policy for value setting, given the celebrity status of pro-football in our society. The new policy is still very far from what should be in place in all professional sports organizations - a "ZERO TOLERANCE OF DOMESTIC VIOLENCE." While there are some very minor criminal acts of domestic violence with no physical injury, first offenses can be very serious, even deadly. If it can be proven that Ray Rice knocked his fiancée unconscious, Mr. Goodell should have this NFL player face the new policy, which could indeed have this athlete banned from the NFL, effective immediately. Whether a professional football player or not, a perpetrator should be banished from the NFL for the one year period for a serious first offense, with a presumption of no reinstatement. I believe knocking your fiancé unconscious falls into the category of a serious injury. Commissioner Goodell needs more education in the area of domestic violence and the risk of repeat offenders. He needs a "No Tolerance Policy" on domestic violence.

Unfortunately, I do believe what happened to Ray Rice could happen here. If Ray Rice had been in North Carolina, he may have been given the option to receive some kind of counseling and dismissal of the criminal charges for a first offense.

Dear Readers,

ZERO TOLERANCE OF DOMESTIC VIOLENCE: I have given considerable thought to the NFL domestic violence problem recently. We are even faced with a current problem with a member of the Carolina Panthers. Beginning in high school, continuing into college and professional sports, each sports participant, where we are teaching hitting and aggression, should receive regular education classes on celebrity conduct, which includes training on domestic violence and violence generally.

Update: Thankfully, the Panther in question, Ed Hardy, moved to Dallas. His conviction was overturned as the witness did not show.

◆ DATING AND DOMESTIC VIOLENCE

Dear Carolyn,

I am a new lady to the dating scene. I have been separated for about six months. I am so taken back by the violent death of the Reedy Fork Elementary school teacher, Ms. Tanner. How can a woman protect herself from dating someone with a domestic violence background, like this Mr. Smith apparently had? He even had a warrant out for him in Arkansas for domestic violence, according to media reports.

Concerned

~ Carolyn Answers...

Dear Concerned,

First, you should be very concerned. Many domestic batterers do not come across at first as domestic violence perpetrators. They can be sweet as honey, until....So what do you do? You need to research.

Before you go out with a guy where you are going to be alone with him, check him out. It is helpful to find out how long the guy has been in Guilford County, and where was he before then. The first trip you want to make in your research is to the Guilford County Courthouse. In the Clerk of Court's office you can determine whether your "guy" has been the defendant in any domestic violence action in Guilford County, any assault on a female action, or a party to a domestic action. Read the files. These are public records and you are entitled to read them.

If you find such files with allegations of domestic violence, wherein the guy was found guilty, you need to consider not getting involved. Evaluate the seriousness of the allegations, and whether there were many incidents or only one. Also, evaluate whether the situation was one minor incident at the time of separation when tempers are flaring, without a history of violence attached to the incident. I think almost anyone can get mad enough under strained circumstances to do something a little irrational.

If the guy was not found guilty, you want to investigate further and be watchful. A guy can be falsely accused, but a guilty guy can also win sometimes. For example, did his ex-wife simply set up a situation to gain control of the house? This happens, unfortunately, which makes judges sometimes skeptical of domestic violence plaintiffs, who abuse the system. This abuse of the system hurts the legitimate plaintiffs.

If the guy has moved around, check with a licensed private investigator to do a statewide or a national criminal background check. If only Ms. Tanner had done this, then she might have found the Arkansas warrant.

I took a quick trip to the courthouse in writing this answer to see if I could find anything on Angelo Smith, Ms. Tanner's boyfriend, in Guilford County. Well, to no surprise, he was the defendant in a domestic violence action here in 2011, according to the files at the Guilford County Courthouse. On July

20, 2011, his former wife, the plaintiff, said that he had caused her extreme emotional distress and bodily harm by overreacting. The judge in the first hearing found that there was escalation in verbal, emotional and physical abuse, and further found that the plaintiff was increasingly fearful of what the defendant might do to her. "He sees no wrong in the way he is treating her and has said so." The Guilford County Sheriff could not serve Mr. Smith, who apparently had a Wendover Avenue address at that time. It appears the 50B was never served on him, notwithstanding concerted effort by the Guilford County Sheriff to serve him.

Would this have made a difference to Ms. Tanner if she had researched him at the courthouse? One can only hope that all of you entering the dating world will make a perhaps life-saving trip to the courthouse to find out background information.

◆ ANIMAL TORTURE

Dear Carolyn,

I am a 35-year-old woman with two small children (a daughter and a son), a puppy, and a cat. I am now separated. My "ex-husband" kicks and tortures the puppy, and I do not know why. The puppy cries and then the children, who witness the violence, cry. It is a mess. The cat usually manages to get away. Then my "ex-husband" yells at the kids and hits them too. I am so glad he is gone, but I worry about this monster I was married to. I worry about how he will treat our children when I am not around, especially when he is drinking. Now he wants visitation with the puppy and the children. What can I do?

Tortured

~ Carolyn Answers...

Dear Tortured,

As I read your letter and think about the horrific abuse that the dog "Toby" has endured as depicted recently in local media, I think that people (and judges) need to understand more about the mentality of persons who will abuse animals. It is typical for animal abusers to simply be abusers, particularly of the vulnerable persons and animals in the abuser's life.

First, here are a few things about persons who abuse animals and children.

Generally, the abuser is replicating a pattern the abuser learned somewhere. Further, the abuse is generally a method of "control" of someone or something. Of course, there is a continuum of abusers, all of which are serious. The least serious (but still serious) are those abusers who merely need some education and counseling to understand the abuse should stop. Perhaps anger management counseling also helps. The most serious situations include where an abuser is a pedophile and uses the animal abuse to control a child victim, who will submit to sex to avoid a beloved pet from being maimed or killed.

You are correct to take the abuse of the animals and your children seriously. All abuse should be taken very, very seriously. It is certainly something to be watched carefully. I do hope you have some pictures or video of what has happened in your home, because likely the abuser will deny, deny, deny. You should document, document, document.

You need to tell the judge in your custody case about the animal abuse and the abuse of the children. I would ask the judge to require the husband to have a mental health evaluation and engage in counseling concerning the abuse, at the very least. You may even consider having the court do a custody evaluation with a psychologist to evaluate the fitness of each parent as a caregiver for the children.

Good that the cat gets away, but the poor puppy.... The puppy is likely marital property to be handled in your property division. He is likely asking for the visitation with the puppy as an additional way to control you in your marital dissolution case. I do not think you will have a problem getting the judge to award the puppy and the cat to you in the property division. Our former Chief Judge Bruce Morton, in Guilford County, use to say in dog cases that the dog should be brought to the courtroom, let loose, and we'll see who the dog runs to. The dog will run to the person he loves.

You will want to try some counseling for yourself to understand patterns of abuse and control. Since your children have witnessed the abuse and have been a part of the violence, counseling would assist them also. Unfortunately, without some intervention these patterns of abuse move from generation to generation.

◆ TEXTING AND STALKING

Dear Carolyn,

My ex-spouse is harassing me with emails and text messages. This ex is saying very mean, nasty things and calling me names. It just won't stop. I hate to give up my cell phone number and my email address, as it would be quite complicated to change. I feel threatened. It's like I am being followed all the time. My ex always seems to know where I am. I still have my cell phone from the marriage. Is it possible there is something planted in the phone? What can I do?

Feeling Threatened

~ Carolyn Answers...

Dear Feeling Threatened,

The digital revolution and cyber warfare is unfortunately part of the current landscape in divorce cases. Wiretapping, spoofing, key logging, and GPS tracking, along with any other imaginable surveillance goes on in divorce cases, even though much of it may be illegal. The National Security Agency or NSA with its Orwellian methods has set the model for the way some spouses and ex-spouses conduct a divorce case. You, as a person going through a divorce cannot simply say, I am not a tech person; you must be knowledgeable to protect yourself and your privacy. The laws and divorce courts have not totally caught up with cyber warfare. Just think, eight of the nine justices of the US Supreme Court do not even use email on a regular basis. That being said, I have three thoughts for your specific situation.

First, your situation may fall into the category of cyberstalking. Cyberstalking is actually a North Carolina crime under NCGS 14-196.3. Under this statute it is unlawful for a person to use email or a cell phone to "communicate to another repeatedly, whether or not conversation ensures, for the purpose of abusing, annoying, threatening, terrifying, harassing, or embarrassing any person." This is a Class 2, misdemeanor.

Second, you also may consider a 50B, as a pattern of continuous harassment can be domestic violence. You would take your evidence of the harassment and go to the courthouse and tell the Clerk of Court that you are interested in a 50B. They will give you forms to fill out, and then you go before a judge who will assess your evidence and decide if a protective order should be entered.

Please, please tell the judge how you feel. If you are scared or frightened, please describe this fully, as not doing this might cost you the protection you need. The first order is good for 10 days, and then there is a hearing where your ex can present his side of the matter. The court will, at this ten day hearing, decide on whether to give you a protective order for up to a year. If you get the protective order or 50B, you can then simply call the police and your ex will be locked up for contacting you. The domestic violence laws need to be strengthened in this area of cyberstalking to catch up with the times, but this is a pattern of harassment under the existing law, in my opinion.

Third, there may be some practical things you can do, such as blocking texts or emails. Your phone service and computer service providers may have a solution for blocking. If your ex was ever the administrator on your cell phone account, go to your cell service provider and have your phone checked for this problem.

We do not yet have the Guilford County Family Justice Center, but hopefully it is coming very soon to our community. If we had this Center today, you could discuss your problem with skilled law enforcement and other skilled professionals for one stop shopping relief. Good luck to you.

◆ HOT CARS AND KIDS LEFT ALONE

Dear Carolyn,

I have been reading the horrid stories about children being left in hot cars. I also have been troubled by my next door neighbor leaving her seven-year-old son alone this summer while she goes to work. I have seen this mother lock the door when she leaves in the morning with the child apparently inside. I do think the seven-year-old has a cell phone. I don't like this situation for the seven-year-old who just finished first grade. Is there anything I can do or should do?

Danger Lurking Next Door

~ Carolyn Answers...

Dear Danger,

Ohhhhhh! It is a crime to leave a child under eight years of age unattended. Further, a child under age eight cannot be left locked up, as this is also a crime. Children under eight years of age must be left with a supervisor of suitable age and discretion. The parent can and will be prosecuted. The placement in the law of this statute is interesting as it is presented as a "fire protection" for little children. However, I do believe that leaving an unattended child under eight in a car would be a crime under this statute as well. (North Carolina General Statutes 14-318.)

The statute does not define further the age of discretion necessary to be a supervisor (babysitter) but what a parent has to do is assess the child's ability and maturity to deal with an emergency. Fort Bragg has military guidelines that are obviously not law but provide some good information. At Fort Bragg, a child cannot be left alone until the child has completed fourth grade. In fifth and sixth grade, a child may be left for up to two hours alone; in grades seven and eight up to four hours alone; ninth and tenth up to six hours alone; and after age sixteen, overnight alone.

Another issue that arises in this area is when can a child babysit another child? North Carolina does not have a law on this, other than we know that a child under eight cannot be left alone. But, this certainly does not imply, in my opinion, that an eight-year-old should be the caretaker of a younger sibling.

We all are reminded of the Randolph County deaths where the Mother locked the outside door of her three-year-old and five-year-old sons' bedroom and a fire broke out killing the two sons. Mother escaped the fire but was charged with manslaughter of her two sons. How very tragic.

So what should you do about the seven-year-old next door? First, you should call Social Services immediately and report this neglect of this seven-year-old. Informants to Social Services are kept confidential. Second, call the police and tell them the situation and ask them to do a "wellness" check.

Thank you for your concern for this child.

◆ 50CS: FORMER WIFE AND NEW WIFE

Dear Carolyn,

The ex-wife of my new husband is constantly calling my cell phone, following me in my car, and making faces at me at the children's soccer game. I get texts from her calling me names. She even threatened to come to my work. I feel intimidated. Can I get a 50B for domestic violence and harassment?

Harassed

~ Carolyn Answers...

Dear Harassed,

You may be able to get a 50-C, not a 50-B. A 50-B is a domestic violence protection order that can be obtained if you have certain types of relationships with the defendant. Unfortunately, 50-Bs do not cover relationship problems between a former wife and a new wife. Typically, 50-B relationships are romantic relationships or parent-child type relationships.

You are eligible to get a 50-C against your husband's ex-wife. Essentially, a victim (you) under the 50-C statute: "Victim.—A person against whom an act of unlawful conduct has been committed by another person not involved in a personal relationship with the person as defined in N.C.G.S. 50B-1(b)." N.C.G.S. 50C-1(8).

You certainly have facts that suggest a 50C might be appropriate. Harassment, intimidation and stalking, along with physical assault (not suggested by your facts) are all reasons for a 50C.

The process starts with the filing of a complaint (a lawsuit) at the courthouse, much like the procedure for a 50B. In fact, in Guilford County, the 50Bs and 50Cs are heard in the same courtroom on the same days. The defendant will not likely be at the first hearing, normally called an *ex parte* hearing. You will be the only one there and will tell your story, which should be much like "shooting a fish in the proverbial barrel." You can seek the help of an attorney, particularly if you feel frightened by the thought of speaking in a courtroom. If the judge agrees that you qualify for a 50C, you will be given an order good for 10 days.

At the end of the 10 days, there will be a hearing where both sides will be heard. If the court grants your 50C, the court can give you many forms of relief, including but not limited to the following: (1) an order to stop stalking (following) you; (2) an order to cease harassment (making the faces); (3) an order to not contact you by telephone, written communications, or other electronic means; (4) order the defendant to refrain from entering your place of employment; and (5) order your attorney fees.

The soccer game itself may be the hardest to deal with, particularly if the child playing soccer is the child of your defendant. The court could certainly order the defendant not to interfere with you at the soccer game. If the child who plays soccer is your child and unrelated to the defendant in any way, ask the judge to ban this crazy woman from the soccer games.

CHAPTER SEVEN

Property Division

◆ GENERAL OVERVIEW

The Court (unless settled by agreement any time after separation) will divide the property owned by you and your spouse. You MUST have a claim for equitable distribution pending on the date of the absolute divorce, or your rights are gone. In North Carolina, this process is described as "Equitable Distribution of Marital Assets".

There are three types of property that must be considered.

a. "Separate property" includes all property owned by either spouse before the marriage or property acquired during the marriage by one spouse by inheritance or gift from a third party. A gift from one spouse to the other during the marriage is marital property unless the donor states at the time of the conveyance that it is intended to be separate property.

b. "Marital Property" includes property presently owned that was acquired during the marriage except property determined to be "separate property." "Marital property" includes all vested pension and retirement benefits acquired during the marriage and prior to separation.

c. "Divisible property" is relatively new. Divisible property is property subject to equitable distribution upon divorce and is defined as real and personal property that includes the appreciation and diminution in value of marital property and other divisible property acquired as a result of actions of the parties during the marriage but before separation, passive income from marital property received after separation and increases in marital debt including finance charges and interest related to marital debt.

The law further creates a presumption that an in-kind distribution of marital or divisible property is equitable, but allows this presumption to be rebutted by the greater weight of the evidence, or by evidence that the property is a closely held business entity or is otherwise not susceptible of division in-kind.

◆ INHERITED REAL PROPERTY (LAND)

Dear Carolyn,

I inherited a family farm. I have never put my spouse's name on the farm. We are separating. Do I have to pay my spouse anything for the farm in the property division?

Separating

~ Carolyn Answers...

Dear Separating,

Luckily, you have not put your estranged spouse on the deed to the inherited family farm, which would have converted the property to marital, presumptively... "There are a different set of facts that need to be reviewed.

If you or your spouse added value to the farm during the marriage out of marital time or marital money, there are perhaps another set of issues that could create a mix of marital and separate property. For example, if you added a barn and your ex built it and the materials were purchased with marital money, then there is a marital component, perhaps. Even paying the property tax bills out of marital property can create concerns.

Generally, the best course of action is to keep separate property you inherited totally separate in all regards, even with regard to the payment of property taxes and insurance. I would need more facts to address your situation more specifically.

◆ TITLE TO REAL PROPERTY IN ONLY ONE SPOUSE'S NAME

Dear Carolyn,

I have a family member who is separated. Before the separation, this person purchased a house with the deed only in her name and the deed of trust in both names. How will the courts view this property for equitable distribution? My family member thinks that since the property is only in her name that the other party has no rights under equitable distribution. Can you explain the difference between Deed and Deed of Trust?

Family Member

~ Carolyn Answers...

Dear Family Member,

This is a very interesting and quite technical question. So, thank you for writing. I'll start first with the definitions of deed and deed of trust.

A deed is the ownership or title documents; by analogy, your car title is a title document for a car like a deed is the title document to your home. Thus, the deed states who owns the home, and generally on the deed the owner is referred to as the grantee. This ownership document (deed) is registered at the Register of Deeds in North Carolina.

A deed of trust is the security for the debt or Promissory Note. When you buy a home or get an equity line on your home, you sign a Promissory Note to the lender. At the time of borrowing, you also sign a document called a deed of trust as security (a lien); if you do not pay the Promissory Note, the signatures on the deed of trust allow the lender to foreclose on the home and take the home away from you. If you examine the deed of trust, you will notice that the lender is the beneficiary of the deed of trust, and that there is a trustee. It is the trustee that forecloses if the Note is not paid. When the Note is completely paid, the lender is required to cancel the deed of trust on the public record at the Register of Deeds. We are one of about twenty states that use the "deed of trust" system. The majority of states use a "mortgage" system.

Because spouses have marital rights in a home, both spouses must sign the deed of trust generally, so that in the event of failure to pay the Promissory Note, the lender can foreclose or take the property away. Otherwise, even if only one spouse owned the property and that same spouse was the only person on the Promissory Note, the lender would not be able to foreclose because of the marital rights under state law of the other spouse. Therefore, it is customary for both spouses to sign the deed of trust, which is also recorded at the Register of Deeds.

Now, let's address your particular question concerning equitable distribution. Equitable Distribution classifies property as marital, separate, and divisible. In your situation, the house was purchased after marriage and before separation. Marital property, simply stated, is property acquired between the date of marriage and the date of separation, and not acquired as a result of an inheritance, family gift or is not separate or divisible property. Thus, we have to ask the questions of where the down payment came from and where are the payments for the Promissory Note coming from. If the down payment and the Note payments are coming from some source, such as an inheritance or property owned before marriage, there is an argument that the property is separate property. Otherwise, the home you described is classic marital property to be divided in the equitable distribution or property division in the case.

However, this is not the end of the story even if there is some separate property involved. Since there is a deed of trust, there is debt. It is highly likely that this debt was paid, probably monthly, during the marriage. Those debt payments were made up of interest and principal. To the extent the debt was reduced during the marriage out of earnings made during the marriage, that debt reduction amount can be divided in equitable distribution. For example, if the debt went from $100,000 to $76,000, there would be $24,000 of marital property to divide at equitable distribution.

Further, even if separate, did the home appreciate during the marriage? If so, the $24,000 would also be entitled to appreciation proportionate to the overall appreciation of the home.

There may also be other factors to consider, such as the following: Were there improvements or renovations during the marriage? Does the non-owner spouse need the home because of custody of the children? Does the non-owner need possession as part of an alimony claim? Consider all of these and good luck to your relative.

Thanks for the question. If you have more facts on the source of the down payment and the monthly payments, please feel free to write again.

◆ CLOSELY-HELD BUSINESS

Dear Carolyn,

I am involved in an equitable distribution and I have a closely-held business started by my father, who still owns the majority of the business. Eight years ago, my father gave me 25 percent of the business. I am now separated. What can I expect in my divorce case related to my closely held business? What is the process for valuing it? Can she get any of my stock in the business?

Stock Holder

~ Carolyn Answers...

Dear Stock Holder,

You ask a complex, but very interesting, question. Rest assured that she cannot get any of the actual stock in your business. The stock itself is separate property because it was given to you by your father.

However, there may be a component of marital value if there is active appreciation. There must be growth in the value of your 25 percent for there to be active appreciation. With the recession and the short length of time you have owned your business, there may be no appreciation, which is the first position you should review.

There may be two types of appreciation of separate property: 1) active and 2) passive. Passive appreciation is growth related to inflation and other market forces, as defined in the famous equitable distribution and divorce case involving Bruton Smith and his ex-wife over the Charlotte Motor Speedway and some car dealerships. You will want to build your case around your business growth, if any, being related to forces beyond your control, such as inflation. Passive appreciation of separate property is NOT divided in a divorce.

Active appreciation of separate property is valued in a divorce and relates to growth related to active participation in the business. You do not say what you do for the business, but if you are the decision maker and the business grows, then the value related to that growth is divided in the divorce either by giving the other spouse more of some other asset, such as the home, or giving the other spouse an offsetting cash award called a distributive award.

How much growth of a separate property business is active and how much is passive is calculated by a business appraiser and presented to the court in the form of expert testimony. The calculation can be quite complex. Your attorney would work with your business valuator to determine the best way to present the value of the active and passive appreciation of your separate property business.

◆ PREMARITAL AGREEMENTS AND THE FAMILY BUSINESS

Dear Carolyn,

My daughter is getting married in 2014. We have a family business and my daughter works in the business; she is not yet an owner. She may receive an ownership interest soon. Is a premarital agreement appropriate for her, even though she is only 25? When should she bring this up with her fiancé?

Practical Parent

~ Carolyn Answers...

Dear Practical Parent,

Yes, a premarital agreement is appropriate if you want to protect family business assets in the unfortunate event of a future divorce or for estate planning issues. Since your daughter works in the business, her active efforts in growing a family business become marital property and thus, distributable in the divorce (to the extent of active appreciation) in a divorce. If you do not want this result, then a premarital agreement is the solution.

When should one bring up a premarital agreement? My advice is to bring the premarital agreement up as soon as the relationship is very serious, so that if signing a premarital agreement is a problem, no one goes deeper into the relationship. Bringing up the premarital agreement might go something like this: The couple is sitting around watching television and the topic of a premarital agreement comes up on the television program. You daughter non-chantingly says: "my family typically has premarital agreements." This is probably easier in the second marriage, so a first marriage has to be handled more carefully and tactfully.

In the end, it is the couple's decision on the premarital agreement; first marriages can become quite emotional on the issue. You, as the parents, control the assets, and if you cannot get your child's cooperation on the premarital agreement, then there are trusts that can be created to help with divorce and estate planning. Please seek a qualified family law specialist for the premarital agreement and an estate planning specialist for trusts, who also might consult with the family lawyer.

◆ THE ENGAGEMENT RING

Dear Carolyn,

I am separated. We were only married two years before separating. She is having an affair. I bought my wife a huge engagement ring, which I gave to her before the wedding. I still owe $25,000 on the ring, which was borrowed before we got married. We paid on the ring during the marriage out of my earnings. My ex will not give back the ring. What are my options?

Help Me!

~ Carolyn Answers...

Dear Help Me,

Ouch! The good news is that the affair ("illicit sexual misconduct") should bar her from alimony. You cannot get alimony if you have committed illicit sexual misconduct, unless the other spouse also had an affair.

The bad news is that the definition of marital property for purposes of asset division are assets that are acquired between the date of marriage and the date of separation. The engagement ring you describe does not fall in this category as it was acquired before the marriage. Unfortunately, she keeps the ring in all likelihood.

Now, let's discuss the debt on the ring. Unfortunately, since the debt was acquired before marriage, the debt---like the ring—is not marital. However, you have the option of claiming the debt as a factor for an unequal division of marital property given that she has the ring and you have the debt. The situation seems fundamentally unfair and thus, the judge may consider this inequity.

You may want to consider a lawsuit against the paramour for alienation of affection and criminal conversation. The monetary award you might receive could help pay off the debt on the ring. This seems only fair since the other guy now has the girl with the big ring. Make him pay this way.

The biggest factor against you in the alienation of affection case is that the marriage was short, and juries tend not to give big awards when the marriage in question was short.

Next time, consider a premarital agreement regarding all economic issues. Good luck!

CHAPTER EIGHT

Social Services and Child Protective Services

◆ HANDLING BULLYING

Dear Carolyn,

I have a case going on with the Guilford County Department of Social Services. The social worker advised me not to get an attorney, and that it would be worse for me if I got an attorney, and that I don't need one anyway. I feel this was a threat, and that I might lose my child if I get an attorney. Can I get an attorney? Should I get an attorney?

Feeling Threatened

~ Carolyn Answers...

Dear Threatened,

You need an attorney, in my opinion, most any time you are dealing with the Guilford County Department of Social Services. The comments below do not reflect on the many great social workers who truly love working with the entire family unit and truly seek to do good things for the entire family, recognizing that the child in question is part of a family unit and an extended family unit. They also deal with difficult situations, but dealing with difficult situations day in and day out can lead a social worker to burn out. Burnout, as well, can lead to bullying.

There are two things wrong with a social worker advising someone not to get an attorney, in my opinion. First, only an attorney licensed in North Carolina can make an accurate assessment of whether you need an attorney and what the legal issues really are or might be. In fact, it very well may be legal advice to tell someone that they do not need an attorney, and it is illegal for someone to give legal advice who is not a licensed attorney in the state where the advice is being given.

Second, there is bullying going on here. Yes, I really did say bullying. I think we can agree that bullying is always wrong, can't we? What is bullying? According to "Google", bullying is a verb. Bullying is using "superior strength or influence to intimidate (someone), typically to force him or her to do what one wants." The synonyms are "persecute, oppress, tyrannize, browbeat, harass, torment, intimidate, strong-arm, and dominate." "We can take your child" is an oppressive, dominating statement when made by Social Services and is an intimidation tactic.

Types of bullies are well studied in current literature. One resource is Anton Hout, founder of OvercomeBullying.org. While there are several types of bullies that may be found in organizations such as Social Services. In your situation, I might classify this bully as either a "gatekeeper" bully or a "constant critic" bully.

a. Gatekeeper bullies deny people the resources they need because it makes the gatekeeper's job more difficult. Denying a person an attorney may very well be a needed resource. Having an attorney may make the social worker's job harder, and certainly the social worker will need to behave in front of your witness, the attorney.

b. "Constant critic" bullies seek to destroy the victim's credibility and will do anything to win, including falsify records or any other devious act.

One of the problems is that organizations can develop a "culture of bullying" and not even recognize that the bullying exists within the culture. Outsiders see the bullying, but inside the organization the bullying is viewed as the norm, albeit a very unhealthy norm.

Parents screw up, but no one should be defined by his/her biggest screw-up. We are all "under construction", and no one is perfect with all the answers. The philosophy of Dr. Bob Goff's book, Love Does would set a good tone for Social Services. The effective social worker is the one on the scene with the family with an attitude of love and helpfulness---that of providing a service to a person "under construction". The attitude of "if you don't do ______, we'll take your kids away" is bullying and is not an effective attitude of helpfulness.

So, you are being bullied. What should you do? Report the bullying and hire an attorney to help you.

◆ PARENTAL RIGHTS DOCTRINE OF THE US CONSTITUTION

Dear Carolyn,

Dear Readers:

A question that is frequently asked in family law is "what is meant by cooperation with CPS (Child Protective Services)?" I welcome letters from readers on this topic. My contact information for "Ask Carolyn" is at the end of this article.

~ Carolyn Answers...

The fourteenth amendment of the United States Constitution creates the Parental Rights Doctrine. It is fundamental to our society that parents have the right to raise their children and the average American, I believe, has a longstanding commitment to parents rights. Except in extreme circumstances, parents have the fundamental right to parent a child and decide what is in the best interests of their own child. (This article doesn't address custody disputes between two good parents each of whom has a fundamental right to parent.) This article does address the fundamental rights of parents over Child Protective Services.

In further advancement of the Parental Rights Doctrine, the United States Supreme Court has had moments of brilliance on this issue. For example, in *Troxel v. Granville*, 530 US 57 (2000), the United States Supreme Court aptly stated: "The liberty interest at issue in this case—the interest of parents in the care, custody, and control of their children---is perhaps the oldest of the fundamental liberty interests recognized by this Court."

So where has the societal shift happened that has placed CPS so squarely in the middle of this fundamental right to parent? I believe the shift happened with the passage of the Adoptions and Safe Families Act of 1997 during the Clinton administration. In my opinion, that Act needs to be abolished and we need to return to the Social Worker Model for CPS, as contrasted to the current Law Enforcement Model. The Social Worker Model is "working with others to accomplish a goal". Perhaps the CPS worker would suggest a needed service, such as counseling through Family Services of the Piedmont, a great organization.

The Law Enforcement Model is "compliance" with the determination of CPS in what is in the child's best interest. An example of the Law Enforcement Model is the police officer has a responsibility to cite you for a traffic violation under the law; we must comply with the traffic laws and compliance is not in the discretion of the driver. The Parental Rights Doctrine is trampled when CPS uses the law enforcement model, as parental rights have much discretion under the 14th Amendment and under many Supreme Court cases. With CPS, the "law" is made by each individual social worker and perhaps his supervisor with no standards or statutes; the CPS worker allegedly knows more about the "best interests" of the child than the parents under the current model.

The traditional Social Work Model begins with charity, which is the historic roots of social work. Thus, the traditional model of social services is rooted in the definition of "work with others to accomplish a goal". According to the International Federation of Social Workers, social work should have three key action areas:

First, social work should promote positive social change. Second, social work should provide problem solving in human relationships, and finally, social work should empower people to enhance their own well-being. It is not a model of interference with the family.

The problem is that the traditional Social Work Model is not being followed, and was abandoned, at least *de facto*, with the 1997 Act mentioned above. In fact, it has become quite the national problem. The Social Work Model has been abandoned for some reason for the Law Enforcement Model of "compliance." The Law Enforcement Model of compliance, for example, requires you to stop your car for a flashing red light or place your hands in the air upon request of an officer. Failure to "comply" with the officer can result in criminal prosecution. The Law Enforcement Model has well-defined parameters for police and as long as long enforcement stays within the well-defined parameters, the "compliance" model works for the benefit of society as a whole. While a police officer may step outside of the parameter, Internal Affairs and even the Justice Department have procedures. Where are the parameters for CPS?

Social work cannot utilize a Law Enforcement Model and accomplish the human objectives social work requires. Social work has to be more collaborative, taking people as a "work in progress" toward greater problem solving skills. CPS should not interfere with families in violation of the Parental Rights Doctrine.

This problem of the law enforcement style CPS department is a growing and alarming trend now being pursued in at least one class action lawsuit in California. According to Shawn McMillan, a civil rights class action lawyer who has sued CPS for kidnapping children, says: "County welfare agencies regularly subvert the constitutional rights of parents when there is no danger to the child, and in fact no need to seize the child at all." (From *Courthouse News*). According to McMillan, his suit is one of many class actions planned against US child protection agencies after the 1997 legislation of increasing funding for adopting foster children. It is my understanding that Guilford County gets money for every child removed from a parent and placed for adoption from the natural parents, although I haven't been able to find out the fact of how much Guilford County gets for this activity.

Studies show that children in state custody are up to 600 percent more likely to be neglected, abused and murdered than those left in parental and extended family custody. Families would be safer with the repeal of the Adoptions and Safe Families Act of 1997. There is nothing safe about it.

◆ OPEN COURTS UNDER THE NC CONSTITUTION

Dear Carolyn,

Does what happened in Union County Social Services happen in the Piedmont Triad, and WHY?

Wondering

~ Carolyn Answers...

Dear Wondering,

Clearly, the Social Services and Child Protective Services of Union County, near Charlotte, went terribly awry. It appears from the media that 36 children were placed in foster care or adopted by Dorian Harper and Social Services Supervisor, Wanda Sue Larson, all under the secrecy laws in North Carolina concerning juveniles removed from their biological parents. The case came to public light when an 11-year-old boy in Larson's and Harper's care was found handcuffed to the porch with a dead chicken around his neck. The child had been burned with electrical wire, cut in the face, tied to railroad ties and had his fingernails pulled out with pliers, among other things. All 36 children should be investigated and charges should be made regarding all abuses. But, it is a secret who these 36 children are. The records of how the placements of these 36 children happened is a secret and what judge or judges allowed the placement is also a secret.

The secrecy laws concerning juveniles and their placement need to be repealed almost entirely to protect the juveniles, their families, and to make Social Services transparent and more accountable. The only confidentiality law needed is one that protects the identity (name) of the juvenile in the media. This concept of openness and transparency is well-grounded in North Carolina starting with the North Carolina Constitution.

Section 18 of the North Carolina Constitution states openly, clearly, and candidly as follows: "All courts shall be open." How much clearer our founding fathers, many of whom lost their lives seeking the freedoms we enjoy, could be regarding the dangers of courtroom secrecy. Does the word "star chamber" ring a bell with anyone? Courts every day in Union County and in the Piedmont Triad can and do hold secret sessions in closed, secret courtrooms in juvenile cases where children are removed from biological parents and placed with people like Larson and Harper. Social Services workers like Larson make arbitrary decisions and become the "god's of the best interest of a child" and all in secret. Hopefully, the legislature will study the Union County case and repeal all laws making juvenile matters and decisions secret, except the protection of the identity of the juvenile in the media. Openness and transparency is desperately needed.

From the media, I understand that Charlotte resident Maria Harris, the biological mother of the 11-year-old in the Union County case, is now involved with her son. Makes you wonder if he should never have been removed from her, doesn't it. What was she doing? Well, it is a deep secret in the tombs of the secret records, unless she tells her own story and she should.

CHAPTER NINE

Miscellaneous

CURRENT SPOUSE HAVING AN AFFAIR

Dear Carolyn,

I am pretty sure my husband is having an affair. We are not separated. I saw a text message where she texted him that she loved him. I checked his phone while he was in the shower. Should I confront him? What should I do?

Bewildered by the Text

~ Carolyn Answers...

Dear Bewildered,

First, I am so sorry for your most difficult situation. You need a consultation with a caring and experienced family lawyer and you need to analyze personally what his reaction to the confrontation might be. There are several possible responses to the confrontation. First, he might confess and get back on the right path with your forgiveness. Or, second, he might erase all of the texts and deny the whole situation. Third, he might just leave. Fourth, the confrontation with emotions running high could instigate a situation of domestic violence. I am sure there are other scenarios.

If you think the situation with the other woman might be serious, you will likely be best served by not confronting and seeking further evidence with a private detective; the detective may be able to determine where the "love nest" is. If you have legal access to his computer you might want to have a forensic computer expert copy the hard drive, as there may be emails that have further information. Get some screen shots of the texts if you have legal access to his phone, as you cannot recover this text information from the phone company.

Look for signs of him changing his habits, such as weight loss. Has he become fit and trim in the last 6 months and become a "gym rat"? Does he come home later or leave earlier? Has he purchased some new clothes? Does he go on more frequent business trips?

Personally, I generally do not recommend immediate confrontation over finding one text message as you are unlikely to ever get him to confess to more than you actually have at that moment.

Dear Carolyn,

I think my wife is having an affair. I am devastated. What do I do?

Devastated

~ Carolyn Answers...

Dear Devastated,

First, do not confront her until you have private investigator proof that she is having an affair. We have lots of great detectives who know exactly what to do.

Second, please consult a family lawyer because if your wife has an alimony claim, the affair will block her from getting alimony---so this is very important to you, financially.

Third, do not sleep with her which could constitute forgiveness of her conduct. Have a headache if she wants sex.

Good luck to you! I know how hard this must be during the holidays!

◆ BIGAMY

Dear Carolyn,

Hello. Can you help me? I am a 51-year-old woman who got into a wedded relationship (though celibate and platonic) with this 73-year-old man whom needed my financial help with his social security. It turns out he never divorced his previous wife nor did she divorce him. Mine with him, I've been told, is invalid and does not count, especially since we did not consummate it on the wedding night for I had my period and he was sick and we still haven't since. It's not like that anyway. Trouble is I am currently unemployed and need work which means I need proper and correct ID (picture, as well as the correct social security card) in order to apply for work.

I don't have income to pay a lawyer to stamp our certificate and license invalid or whatever they do to help free the invalid spouse from the one still married to the previous one. How can I get our documents stamped invalid by the courts (the law, lawyers, Judges – whoever) so I will have proof to switch back to my original birth name to get my ID and social security correct in order to fill out applications without income to pay a lawyer?

Are there legal agencies you know of that can and will help me so I can move on?

Also, I have been told the law will not prosecute them for not divorcing unless it had to do with property. Is that true? I do not want to send anyone to jail, I just want to be freed from this falsehood in order to move on with my life.

Dismayed

~ Carolyn Answers...

Dear Dismayed,

I am so sorry. Please stand up for yourself, as you certainly have been duped. You appear from the facts you present to be a victim of the crime of bigamy.

Luckily, you have a cause of action for annulment in North Carolina. Your ground for annulment is governed by North Carolina General Statute 51-3, which states in relevant part: "All marriages...between persons either of whom as a husband or wife living at the time of such marriage...shall be void."

You have to file a complaint and summons (a lawsuit) with the District Court where you live, presumably Greensboro. You need to state in your complaint the following:

a. Name and where the other party lives;
b. Date of the purported marriage and the location of the purported marriage;
c. Children born, of whom there are none under your circumstances, but you need to state this anyway.
d. State the circumstances of the marriage your purported husband had with his actual wife. Attach that marriage license of your purported husband to his actual wife, if possible.
e. You can add that your marriage was never consummated if you wish, but this really doesn't matter under the technical legal statutes, in your situation.
f. State which name you want to use after the annulment;
g. Ask the court to grant you an annulment.

There is no prohibition against you doing this yourself, but it will be a little cumbersome. You will have to write your complaint. The Clerk of Court located at the courthouse will likely give you a Summons to fill out. You will pay a filing fee to the Clerk of Court and give the Sheriff with his fee the Summons and Complaint to give to ("serve") your purported husband. He will have 30 days to answer. He may or may not answer. At any rate, after the 30 days go back to the courthouse and apply for a calendar date for your case to be heard. At the hearing, you should receive a Judgment of Annulment.

You will use this Judgment of Annulment to get all of your documents straightened out like your social security card and your driver's license.

You might check with Legal Aid and see if they will help you. You also might post a request at Elon Law School to see if there is a young lawyer who might do this for you for free ("pro bono"). Call Elon Law and ask for the "pro bono" division.

You are probably describing the crime of "bigamy", which is a Class I felony (North Carolina General Statutes section 14-183). Whether this will be prosecuted is up to law enforcement and the District Attorney, and the prosecution, if any, will be out of your control. However, I will say my gut is that there will not be a prosecution unless you push for one. At any rate, YOU NEED YOUR ANNULMENT, and I strongly urge you to pursue this immediately.

◆ ATTORNEY FEES

Dear Carolyn,

I am short on money, and I am wondering, can I get my estranged husband to pay for my attorney fees? We have been separated four months, and I have filed with the court for property, child support, child custody, and alimony. Can I get attorney fees?

In Need of Fees

~ Carolyn Answers...

Dear In Need of Fees,

Generally, you, as a litigant have a claim for attorney fees in domestic litigation, in certain circumstances prescribed in statutes by the legislature. Fees are discretionary with the judge and results certainly vary from case to case. Here are some general rules (there are nuances not addressed here you should discuss with your family law attorney):

1. **Equitable Distribution (property division):** You cannot get attorney fees, generally. There is a sanction (penalty) provision available for serious delays in the equitable distribution process.
2. **Child Support:** You may receive attorney fees, if you are the recipient and if the other parent was paying inadequate child support at the time you filed for child support.
3. **Custody:** You may receive attorney fees if you are proceeding in good faith.
4. **Post Separation Support and Alimony:** You may receive attorney fees as the recipient of post separation support and alimony.
5. **Domestic Violence:** There is a statutory discretionary attorney fee provision.
6. **Mediation:** Most of the time in Guilford County, when claims are settled in mediation, the parties settle by paying his/her own attorney fees, regardless of the claim(s) being mediated.

◆ PERJURY

Dear Carolyn,

My soon to be ex-wife lied under oath in court for personal gain (money). She over-stated expenses and I am paying P.S.S. Can I charge her with perjury and sue her?

Thanks,
P.J.

~ Carolyn Answers...

Dear P.J.,

Unfortunately, this is a frequently asked question in family law and divorce cases. It seems that, almost always, someone thinks one side or the other is lying. For all readers' information, P.S.S. is Post Separation Support, a temporary form of alimony. The question is as follows: what can you do about the false statement?

This answer will first discuss your allegation of perjury. Then, secondly, the answer will discuss possible civil remedies and suggestions for your divorce.

First, perjury is a very serious crime under N.C.G.S. 14-209 and is a Class F Felony. Perjury is "a false statement under oath, knowingly, willfully and designedly made, in a proceeding in a court of competent jurisdiction or concerning a matter wherein the affiant is required by law to be sworn, as to some matter material to the issue or point in question." *State v. Bright*, 301 N.C. 243 (1949). Further, "it is required that the falsity of the oath be established by the testimony of two witnesses, or by one witness and corroborating circumstances." *State v. King*, 267 N.C. 631 (1966).

In my experience, I have found, practically, that District Attorneys (prosecutors) are reluctant to prosecute perjury cases in divorce situations. However, there is a significant case in 2007 involving a child support matter that is worth discussion; that case is *State v. Denny*, 361 N.C. 662 (2007). In *Denny*, a Father appeared in court for failure to pay child support. The Father filled out an Affidavit of Indigency to obtain a court appointed attorney for free, which would be to the financial benefit of the Father. On the Affidavit of Indigency, the Father wrote "zero" on the line asking about real estate assets. Later, someone uncovered that the Father owned a legal title to real estate with his girlfriend. The Father was prosecuted for perjury and the North Carolina Supreme Court affirmed the conviction.

P.J., if you have the two witnesses or the one witness and otherwise corroborating proof, you should discuss your case with law enforcement and the District Attorney's office. My guess is that you will not likely be successful because you are in a divorce, but the State was successful against Mr. Denny in a child support matter. We would need to know more about your specific facts, and why you think perjury occurred. If you still think you have perjury after reading this response, please write again and include more facts.

Your second remedy is the civil court action you are currently in for Post Separation Support. The good news for you is that Post Separation Support (P.S.S.) by definition is temporary. The judge likely set a fixed term for the P.S.S., such as one year or eighteen months. Alimony is the next step and that is where you have the opportunity to be prepared for the lies. You should do extensive discovery from your ex on her income and expenses from her Affidavit of Financial Standing, which she is required to file for her Alimony claim. In Guilford County, certain documents must also be given to you with the Affidavit of Financial Standing, but these documents will not be sufficient to deal with a liar. You will have to ask additional questions (called interrogatories) and request additional documents (called a production of documents). You can even require your ex to answer questions verbally, under oath, in a deposition.

Finally, if the fraud and misrepresentation to the court is clear and provable, you may have a Rule 60 Motion for Relief from Judgment or Order, if filed within one year of the P.S.S. Order. Your attorney will need to make a strategic call on whether you should file under Rule 60 or simply pursue the alimony, or perhaps both. I do think you are going to need an experienced family lawyer to help you.

◆ SUBPOENA TO COURT

Dear Carolyn,

I just got a subpoena from my neighbor's lawyer to come to court. I really don't want to get involved in this custody mess. Plus, I have to work. I do see the children playing in their yard, and they appear well taken care of. Can't I just write a letter? Do I have to go just because the Sheriff delivered this piece of paper called a "subpoena" to me? Eek!

Frustrated

~ Carolyn Answers...

Dear Frustrated,

Having been personally inconvenienced a few times myself with receipt of a subpoena, I identify with what you are saying. It is a pain to be pulled in other people's court cases. However, we are in a free society and part of being a member of a free society is participation in our system of justice through the courts. Judges must have facts to make good decisions and many of those facts come from good folks, just like you, who have no reason to twist or taint the truth. Whatever you have seen is what you have seen. By what you tell me, you do not have any allegiances to one side or the other.

The letter does not work because the side that is not calling you has the right to cross examine you. The U.S. Constitution gives the rights to litigants to confront witnesses against them. Letters are one-sided and are hearsay.

You should call the attorney to discuss when your testimony might be needed so you can minimize your involvement as much as possible. Also, show your boss the subpoena, so he will excuse you from work.

There are objections you can file to a subpoena and you can read about these on the back of the subpoena itself. The law requires that you be served with details about how to make objections. Read through the back of the subpoena to find out what your rights are regarding objections.

◆ SAME-SEX MARRIAGE

Dear Carolyn,

I just got my citizenship and I am in a same sex marriage with someone who is a citizen of France. I have been hearing about all of these constitutional and unconstitutional issues over same sex marriages in the United States. Can my partner now immigrate here?

Confused

~ Carolyn Answers...

Dear Confused,

First, you are going to need an immigration lawyer for the details of your situation but I can comment from a family law point of view.

From a family law point of view, you are in luck! The United States Supreme Court in *Windsor* found section 3 of the Defense of Marriage Act (DOMA) to be unconstitutional. Thus, U.S. federal agencies are now viewing same-sex marriage in the same way that they view applications for opposite gender spouses. This applies to the way the U.S. Immigration and Naturalization Service (INS) views same sex marriages.

Thus, for purposes of INS, your same sex spouse will be viewed the same way as an opposite sex spouse, with regard to such things as work, study, international exchange, or legal immigrant status. These are typically referred to as visa status or green card status. Also, any stepchildren you acquire though the same sex marriage will be treated the same way.

To achieve these benefits, your marriage must have been valid and legal wherever the marriage took place.

I wish you both the best in your future together.

◆ SEEKING COUNSEL

Dear Carolyn,

You answered all my questions about how to obtain an increase in a court ordered alimony agreement in your article several weeks ago. Now that I am trying to begin the process, I have been unable to obtain an attorney. The main excuse for them not taking my case is that their fees are high and they don't think I can pay. I have obtained financial support from my son. He will be footing the bill. Everyone wants to recommend someone else but not themselves. What's a body to do in this case? Would appreciate hearing from you in a future article.

Seeking Counsel

~ Carolyn Answers...

Dear Seeking Counsel,

The selection of a family lawyer that is a fit for you and your case is very, very important. For many, a family law matter is a person's first encounter with a lawyer. It is important that you be comfortable with the lawyer you select. It is preferred by me that the lawyer and the client have compatible styles of dealing with dispute resolution.

How do you get started with your case?

My preference is that you call the office of a family law specialist and ask the person who answers (typically not an attorney) for an initial appointment, commonly referred to as an initial consultation. A family law specialist has at least five years' experience in family law, has taken a second bar exam just in family law, as well as had other peer review credentials. There are also good family lawyers who are not specialists, so ask a lot of questions about experience at the initial consultation.

The first phone call is important for obtaining an appointment. You will likely be ask who the opposing party is so that the law firm can run a "conflict check." I would not expect the intake paralegal/assistant on this initial call to go over the details of the case. The appointment is scheduled to go over the details. The part of your question that is a little baffling to me is that your question suggests there are all kinds of fee discussions going on with the call to make an appointment. Stick to simply making the appointment and finding out what the fee for that initial consultation is.

I believe that many attorneys who practice family law start with an initial consultation with a fee for the initial consultation. Call a family law specialist or other family lawyer and ask for an appointment and agree to pay the fee for the appointment. There are some lawyers who give free initial consultations, as well.

Typically, as part of that first appointment future fees, retainers, and/or security deposits will be discussed and you will likely be offered a written fee agreement that you can take home and review. If you like that attorney, you can return the signed fee agreement, required retainer and/or security deposit. You will then be a client and have additional meetings.

Be prepared for the first meeting with any documents you have that relate to your case, such as agreements with your ex-spouse, court orders, and financial records such as tax returns.

◆ SEPARATION

Dear Carolyn,

My wife and I have been married 20 years. Our child is graduating from high school this year, and we are miserable. We own a home with lots of debt and we cannot afford to separate without selling our home first. We both work, but there simply is not enough money to maintain two households without first selling the house. Is there any way we can declare ourselves separated and maintain the same household until the house sells? Why is the North Carolina waiting period for divorce a year? I hear that one year is a long time as compared to other states. Can we settle our property now? We have retirement, cars and furniture, along with the house?

Wanting to Separate

~ Carolyn Answers...

Dear Wanting,

Generally, North Carolina requires 365 days of separation, with the intent of one spouse to live separate and apart forever, before a spouse may apply to the court for an absolute divorce. Separation in this state means, literally that the spouses, during separation, must have separate residences and essentially, conduct themselves as single for the entire 365 days. Isolated incidences of sexual intercourse, such as a weekend at the beach with an estranged spouse, do not start the 365 day period over.

The answer to your first question is that you cannot declare separation and maintain the same household until the house sells under North Carolina law. North Carolina has strong pro marital advocates in our legislature, as compared to other States. Some States, such as Alabama, allow spouses to live together through the date of the divorce and the division of property. Other States have much shorter waiting periods of living apart, such as six weeks. North Carolina, if anything, is going in the opposite direction of the national trend which is to recognize the desire of a party to a marriage to go his or her separate way, without regard to whether the spouses are under the same roof.

The practical solution for you is to list and sell your home. When the home sells, you and your spouse simply go your separate ways.

The good news is that in North Carolina, spouses can settle equitable distribution (property division) by a notarized agreement at any time before, during or after the marriage. Yes, you can settle your property division now, while you are waiting on the house to sell. Of course, the agreement will need provisions for who pays the debt, property taxes and insurance on the house until it sells and how the proceeds will be divided when the home sells.

◆ SELLING REAL ESTATE IN AN ESTATE

Dear Carolyn,

I have been married to my wife almost two years. Recently, and unfortunately, her grandmother passed away. Her grandmother had no immediate means to pay for funeral and burial services. The costs were paid by my wife and me on our credit card. The family has considerable land assets, but it is in her grandmother and multiple siblings' name. My wife will inherit a portion of her grandmother's land (split with my wife's uncle). No one in the family has the means to buy us out, and, as is often the case, there is no reachable agreement by the family to divide the land. Is there any way to sell off some or all of what my wife is entitled to help reimburse us for the costs of the funeral and burial services?

Thanks for your helpful insight,
Jon D.

~ Carolyn Answers...

Dear Jon D,

We have a solution for you! The property can be sold to pay funeral and burial expenses, but there are several steps you must follow.

The answer assumes there was no Will, as a Will was not mentioned.

First, your spouse will need to go to the Clerk of Court, Estates Division at the Guilford County Courthouse if the grandmother died in Guilford County and open an estate file for the grandmother. If the grandmother died in another county, you need to open the estate file in that county. Someone is going to have to qualify as the administrator of the estate. Your wife, as a granddaughter may apply; others may also apply, but hopefully they will not.

The administrator will be given "Letters of Administration", showing that the administrator can conduct business for the estate.

Second, the administrator will run a creditor's notice as required by the statute and the Clerk's office. The Clerk's office should be helpful to explain this further when you appear in that office.

Third, file the funeral and burial expenses and proof of your payment in the grandmother's file at the Estates Division at the courthouse.

Fourth, the administrator is required to tally the bills of the estate for all creditors (those that respond to the creditor's notice and others with outstanding invoices related to the grandmother). Your bill would be among these bills.

Also, the administrator is required to collect all assets, such as a bank account belonging to the deceased grandmother, a social security check, life insurance, and personal property such as a diamond ring.

Finally, we know there is real estate. If the other assets of the estate are not enough to pay all creditors, the land will have to be sold to pay the creditors, including you. According to Bradley L. Jacobs, a local Estate Planning and Probate Law Specialist, "it is sometimes necessary to have the judicial sale to pay creditors and may be the only way to repay the funeral expenses. It is unfortunate though, as the judicial sale does require a hearing to determine if there are insufficient assets. An appraisal will be needed, and a petition to approve the sale." It may be hard to accomplish all of this without an attorney for the estate, but approved attorney fees to do this will also be an expense of the estate and paid from the estate.

I suggest you and your wife start with a visit to the Clerk of Court, Estates Division in the county where the grandmother died. Good luck!

◆ DIVORCE RECOVERY TIPS

Divorce Recovery Tip:

Learn to exercise self-control. Divorces are emotional and sometimes a person going through divorce can get out of touch with self-control.

Divorce Recovery Tip:

Find "joy" this weekend! What is "joy" to you? Write down ten things that give you "joy" and do some of them.

IF YOU HAVE QUESTIONS:

Send your questions on family law and divorce matters to "**Ask Carolyn...**" at askcarolyn@rhinotimes.com, or P.O. Box 9023, Greensboro, NC 27427. Please do not put identifying information in your questions. Note that the answers in "Ask Carolyn" are intended to provide general legal information, and the answers are not specific legal advice for your situation.

A subtle fact in your unique case may determine the legal advice you need in your unique case. Also, please note that you are not creating an attorney-client relationship with Carolyn J. Woodruff by writing or having your question answered by "**Ask Carolyn...**" "**Ask Carolyn...**" will be a regular column, but not necessarily weekly, and may use hypothetical questions.

The Seven Nights of Santa

AUTHORS

DWIGHT A. ENSLEY AND CAROLYN J. WOODRUFF

The Seven Nights of Santa is a holiday book for small children, their parents, grandparents, and caregivers. Today's family units encompass a large variety of family forms. Many children do not live with both of their natural parents. This leads to much stress and dispute during the holidays, particularly as to which house Santa will deliver toys and other presents.

In *The Seven Nights of Santa*, Captain Green Eyes resolves the issue for his little Cupcake Buddies and for Cupcake Buddies everywhere. For seven nights, Santa can come to different houses and deliver toys and other presents. With the Santa list for each home in hand, all a child must do is tell Santa what night to come to which home. Each parent, grandparent or caregiver can share with the child the surprises left by Santa under the tree at that home.

Captain Green Eye's mission is to help all the little Cupcake Buddies out there to accept and love their family units regardless of form. We hope this book will bring to you and your Cupcake Buddies more happiness, kindness, understanding, and love.

Cupcake Buddies

Made in the USA
Monee, IL
05 November 2026

67387502R00064